Futurism
Politics, Painting and Performance

University Studies in
the Fine Arts: The Avant-Garde, No. 8

Other Titles in This Series

Futurism

Politics, Painting and Performance

by
Christiana J. Taylor

umi
RESEARCH PRESS

Produced and distributed by
University Microfilms International
Ann Arbor, Michigan 48106

Library of Congress Cataloging in Publication Data

Taylor, Christiana J   1943-
   Futurism.

   (Studies in the fine arts : Avant-garde ; #8)
   Bibliography: p.
   Includes index.
   1. Futurism (Art) 2. Arts, Modern—20th century.
3. Politics in art.   I. Title. II. Series.

NX600.F8T35   700'.9'04   79-24378
ISBN 0-8357-1062-9

CONTENTS

ILLUSTRATIONS

PREFACE

When I began this study in 1970 it seemed to me that the Futurists were a small bellicose group of artists and writers whose impact on the development of Dada and other avant-garde movements should be examined. My information led me to believe that there were certain connections between Futurist methods and the methods of later better publicized groups from which the experimental theatre of today has grown. After four years of research and evaluation I have revised my attitude about the importance of the Futurist movement. I no longer see the movement as a minor event in the development of twentieth century theatre practices but rather as the seminal movement which incorporated the major innovations of non-realistic theatre practices. No other event in the theatrical history of the early part of this century exploded with such vigor and creativity. No other movement accomplished so many innovations and revolutions in the art of the theatre before 1920.

This study does not address itself to the secondary considerations of the impact of Futurism upon twentieth century art and theatre except to suggest these connections and guide the reader to a full understanding of the work which the Futurists undertook. These connections are complex and would involve a comprehensive analysis of each of the movements. Among those modern movements owing a debt to Futurism are: Dada, Surrealism, Bauhaus Theatre, Absurd Drama and Happenings.

Theatre historians have not often taken an interdisciplinary view of the development of the theatre. The discipline of the theatre, encompassing as it does several professional techiques, provides the historian with an already unwieldy field of study without taking on the added complications of the sister arts such as painting, poetry and literature. Nevertheless, these relationships are of vital importance to an understanding of the development of Futurism. Therefore, the present study has involved interdisciplinary research that has focused on the influence which painting and the visual arts has had upon the design of the stage scene, as well as the impact of literary developments upon the text of the theatre. An interdisciplinary study is both invigorating and frustrating since each discipline tends to regard the others as unconnected. Furthermore, there are very few texts which address the interdisciplinary scholar and this absence of written material lends support to the impression that there are no concrete connections between artists and theatre workers, or poets and playwrights. The terms used to identify art movements and theatre movements are frequently the same, as they stem from similar philosophical and artistic attitudes. However, historians rarely provide the reader with an understanding of these similarities and their translation from one discipline to another. Without that understanding, it is difficult to grasp the significance of Futurism, which has been virtually ignored by standard theatre history texts.

Futurism, as this work will demonstrate, has no direct antecedents in the history of the theatre. It is a movement whose visual development preceded a fully realized form of drama or theatre. Hence, the development of the Futurist theatre was enormously influenced by the devices and ideas of the Futurist painters. Indeed, the major figures involved in the formulation of the Futurist theatre were painters, except for Marinetti himself—the founder of the Futurist movement. Therefore, it would be worthwhile to review the art historical developments which influenced the Futurists.

The influence of the Impressionists is evident in the work of the Futurist painters, especially in the Impressionist motif and their fascination with the possibilities of movement and the qualities of light. From the Impressionists the Futurist painters defined the interrelationships between objects and their surroundings, relationships which they extended into the principle of interpenetrability. The Futurists shared with the German Expressionists a desire to fuse themselves with the identities of other objects and milieu in order that they might create a single complex. The influence of the Post-Impressionist technique of divisionism was used with success by the Futurists but with great freedom of brushstroke which defies Seurat and Signac. Finally, the disintegration and rebuilding of forms which the Cubists had been exploring for two years provided another extension of Futurist vocabulary which they turned to their own needs, principally the registering of various states of movement in space which could be described by the repetition of forms on the picture surface.

These influences (and others) which affected the development of the Futurist painters were then translated into an appropriate theatre vocabulary. Hence, the development of the Futurist theatre has much in common with the developments occurring in the visual arts and only secondarily does the Futurist theatre reflect any influence from the development of dramatic art during the years 1900 to 1920. In fact, the Futurist theatre was unique in Europe in its boldness and originality of devices and innovations. The art of the Futurist theatre was not eclectic nor derivative, but grew from the impulses which originated with the work of the painters and were translated by the poets and by Marinetti himself into a theatre aesthetic. The single outstanding influence which can be documented was that of Alfred Jarry, for whom Marinetti had great admiration.

While the Futurist theatre had little in common with any other form of theatre extant during the prewar years, it is significant that the Futurists intended to obliterate all forms of contemporary theatre and to replace the "psychological, sentimental, logical, causal, developmental, symbolic" theatre with a new theatre which would be aggressive, involving and original. The theatre which they accomplished was the product of the innovations which had occurred in the visual arts and literature of the movement. One of the difficulties of recapturing that theatre through research has been that the least important element, the text, is nearly all that is available. Hence, as has been the case often in theatre history, the scholar is left with the most ambiguous aspect of the production from which to restructure the event. However, the available material dealing with performance, painting, and politics gives the researcher a fairly complete view of Futurist theatre.

Finally, the reader may ask why a movement of such consequence and such vigor has been completely ignored by the vast majority of theatre historians. As pointed out in the work which follows, the stigma which was attached to the Futurist movement during the rise and fall of the Axis powers between 1933 and the end of the Second World War cannot be overstated. A movement which had achieved international recognition, which had been copiously imitated and admired throughout Europe and the East, was literally erased from existence by the historians of the post-war period. The Italian government carried out a campaign to censor all research and publication of documents which pertained to the infamous Futurist movement after the First World War. Even today, information about the movement after 1920 is sparse and fragmentary.

Propositions can be set forth for the minimal amount of attention afforded the Futurist theatre in this country before the Second World War when the Futurists were enjoying a considerable vogue in Europe and elsewhere. The central reason seems to be that the documents of the movement concerning theatre were not translated into English, although they were translated into several other languages. Moreover, the attention accorded to other less disquieting groups and individuals was considerable. Gordon Craig, Max Reinhardt, and later Meyerhold and Vakhtangov were the darlings of the American critics and historians who travelled to Europe between the wars to experience the avant-garde. Each of these men was abundantly publicized in English while only two periodicals covered the Futurists in English: one was Gordon Craig's article on the Futurists which appeared in "The Mask" and the other an excellent article which appeared in "Theatre Magazine." It is the author's opinion that the nature of the Futurist theatre was unpleasant and uniquely un-American to those who may have seen it or read of it during those years. The Futurists were so adamantly opposed to the whole spiritual mystique which American men of the theatre were practising with such ardor that it can hardly be wondered that they would reject a theatre which so firmly and audaciously rejected them.

ACKNOWLEDGMENTS

I would like to thank my friend and advisor Dr. John R. Wolcott. He offered me his expertise, his intelligence and his humor without which this would have been a dreary task. I thank Skip, Amy and Alex for their patience and encouragement. Also, I thank Arlene for her friendly assistance.

I

POLITICS

Futurism emerged as a uniquely twentieth century phenomenon, encompassing many art forms and inextricably bound to a concrete political contention. The Futurists were the first artists of this century who pledged themselves to ideological activity and devoted their energies and talents to converting the masses to that ideal, rather than to formalizing and promoting their individual artistic merits. Without patronage or support from any powerful government agency, the Futurists initiated and succeeded in an ideological and artistic revolution which affected most of the western world. Certainly they were the harbingers of a characteristic methodology for movements both political and artistic throughout this century.

The Futurists were a tightly knit, ardently committed amalgam. They used their organization as a resource center. They became expert at the dissemination of propaganda in a variety of forms and through an array of procedures which were a startling innovation when compared with the informality and fluctuation of other contemporary movements and their predecessors. Indeed, their reputation for propaganda virtuosity has been more publicized than their politics.

Historians have paid attention to such aspects of Futurism as painting and sculpture, but no attempt has been made to comprehend the impact of the movement as a decisive political-artistic force, a force which permeated the mass consciousness of Italy and perhaps the world for four years before the first World War. Moreover, most scholars have denied or disregarded the relationship between Futurist political objectives and Futurist art, preferring to treat both aspects as if they were less substantial than other movements such as Dadaism and Surrealism. It is the contention of the present study that many of the premises advocated in Futurist manifestoes between 1909 and 1933 were widely publicized and emphatically affected many diverse artistic and political arenas throughout Europe, Russia, England, America and Japan. Further, the Futurists designed a program in the arts and in politics which predicted developments up to the present.

Unlike Impressionism, Fauvism and Cubism, movements which directly preceded it, Futurism was produced whole cloth as a complete idea and announced publicly in various journals around the major art centers of Europe, England and Russia. In fact, in nearly every respect, Futurism was a considerable departure from the usual tradition of evolving and dissolving art movements whose political implications were slight or non-existent. Futurism did not evolve or emerge from vague concurrent influences, as in the genteel, if hazy,

1

manner of Fauvism and other contemporary movements. Rather, it was created by the poet Filippo Tommaso Marinetti (1876-1944) as a means of legitimatizing the philosophical platform upon which his literary and political activities were based. Marinetti controlled and influenced the movement to such an extent that one cannot consider Futurism without considering its founder.

Filippo Tommaso Marinetti was born in Alexandria, the second son of a wealthy merchant and artistically inclined mother. He grew up in a family of upper middle class gentility where literature and art were highly valued and where wealth made strenuous activity unnecessary.

A biographer speaks of Marinetti's temperament in childhood, which is not unlike that of the grown man twenty years later: "a gentle, volcanic, nostalgic, amazed and sentimental bambinone (big baby)."[1] This is a reliable description of a boy whose essay on Egyptian sunset was marked by his Jesuit teacher with the words, "Surpassed anything Chateaubriand ever wrote,"[2] but who was later expelled for refusing to read anti-Italian accounts of Pope Pius IV which included attacks on Garibaldi. (The reader should understand that it was Garibaldi over whom Marinetti made the issue which resulted in his expulsion, not the Pope.) In 1893 he went to Paris for his baccalaureate; two years later he was in Pavia, then Genoa for a degree in law. Four years later, Marinetti's older brother Leone, considered the more promising of the two boys, died of rheumatic fever in Milan, where the family had moved in 1900 to a "large, appallingly Egyptianized apartment."[3] Marinetti's mother died in 1902, a recluse, and his millionaire father amused himself by hiring young women to read him comparative religion, alternated with erotica, and by visits to the local 'case chiuse'.[4] Marinetti's father died in 1907, leaving his son the apartment and all his money.

In 1905, Marinetti founded the controversial literary review "Poesia" which addressed the problem of stagnation, passéism and mediocrity in the arts and in the Italian nation. It was Marinetti's view that Italy had degenerated into a tourist mogul celebrating its glorious past for the sake of the German antiquarians who emigrated by the thousands each year. His belief that Italian artistic activity had all but perished had been confirmed by his presence at the funeral of Giuseppe Verdi in 1901, the last of the Risorgimenti giants.[5] Marinetti was also present at the state funeral for the poet Carducci, a former senator and Republican of considerable moral authority. Marinetti believed that the deaths of these two internationally recognized figures left only D'Annunzio, the Divine Imaginifico (maker of images), to fill the roles of Italian celebrity, leader for the aspiring young artists at home and prophet-advocate for Italian arts and letters in the twentieth century. Moreover, for D'Annunzio, Marinetti had the most ambiguous personal and professional feelings.

Marinetti had founded his new review with more in mind than a revitalization in the arts. He was cognizant of the evolving national consciousness, long buried beneath the vigorous, if petty, rivalries of the city-states. He was conversant with the workings of a scandal ridden monarchy bent on the pacification of aging revolutionaries and was especially ardent in his opposition to the Catholics and Socialists, two of the most prominent adversaries of the state, who had somehow been absorbed and manipulated into the fabric of the parliamentary system where they were quickly reduced to ineffectual "in-fighting" among themselves.

Marinetti used his magazine to expound and articulate his growing frustration and animosity toward the complaisance and compromise of Victor Emmanuel III's administration, carried out and described principally in the policies of Giovanni Giolitti, King Emmanuel's chief minister from 1903 to 1914. Giolitti's ultimate aim was the pacification of the anarchist and violent groups which had brought about the assassination of Victor Emmanuel's father, King Humbert, in July 1900. To that end he was astonishingly successful, so much so that virtually all dissident elements had been brought under manipulative control via the use of the most flagrant and audacious forms of bribery, coercion, patronage and sheer armed force.[6] Marinetti's position was based on irreconcilable philosophical differences with the ultimate aim of the liberal government as epitomized by Giolitti's policy of internal pacification. However, more than to his disgust with the cult of the past or his impatience with the vacillations of state, Marinetti was dedicated to the concept of nationalism, a concept which was based upon the absolute necessity of a resurgence of Italian political power in an arena where German, French, and English statesmen vied for supremacy and too often dictated policy for all the rest of Europe.

As his political and artistic philosophies evolved in the editions of *Poesia* between 1905 and 1909, Marinetti began to explore the potential for disseminating his ideas. Already a familiar figure in the cafe society of Paris, he had met and become friendly with a number of important literary and artistic figures. Marinetti seems to have been most affected by his friendship with the eccentric, alcoholic young author Alfred Jarry.[7] Marinetti had written his first play *Le Roi Bombance* in admiring imitation of Jarry's *Ubu Roi*. Of the many obvious sources for Marinetti's development as an entrepreneur par excellence none seems to have had such an enormous impact as this friendship. From Jarry, Marinetti learned the efficacy and expediency of arrogance, bombast and buffoonery, means by which one gained attention and acquired a platform in the raucous, extravagant Paris of the 1900's. Marinetti realized and developed his ability to attract an audience by exhibitionist methods. In addition, Marinetti's other literary contacts were extensive and he was able to promote himself and his burgeoning ideology to the front ranks of the literary world. Marinetti was a well considered poet having published in leading literary journals such as "La Voce," "L'Unita," "Il Regno" and "Il Leonardo." As a result of his contacts and talent he was able to launch his movement in a major Paris journal, "Le

Figaro," where the Foundation Manifesto appeared on the front page of the issue of February 20, 1909.

The Foundation Manifesto of Futurism, translated by R.W. Flint, from Le Figaro February 20, 1909.

We had stayed up all night, my friends and I, under hanging mosque lamps with domes of filigreed brass, domes starred like our spirits, shining like them with the prisoned radiance of electric hearts. For hours we had trampled our atavistic ennui into rich oriental rugs, arguing up to the last confines of logic and blackening many reams of paper with our frenzied scribbling.

An immense pride was buoying us up, because we felt ourselves alone at that hour, alone, awake, and on our feet, like proud beacons or forward sentries against an army of hostile stars glaring down at us from their celestial encampments. Alone with stokers feeding the hellish fires of great ships, alone with the black spectres who grope in the redhot bellies of locomotives launched down their crazy courses, alone with drunkards reeling like wounded birds along the city walls.

Suddenly we jumped, hearing the mighty noise of the huge double decker trams that rumbled by outside, ablaze with colored lights,...

'Let's go!' I said. "Friends, away! Let's go!... let's break out of the horrible shell of wisdom and throw ourselves like pride-ripened fruit into the wide contorted mouth of the wind! Let's give ourselves utterly to the Unknown, not in desperation but only to replenish the deep wells of the Absurd!'....

Manifesto of Futurism

1. We intend to sing the love of danger, the habit of energy and fearlessness.

2. Courage, audacity, and revolt will be essential elements of our poetry.

3. Up to now literature has exalted a pensive immobility, ecstasy, and sleep. We intend to exalt aggressive action, a feverish insomnia, the racer's stride, the mortal leap, the punch and the slap.

4. We affirm that the world's magnificence has been enriched by a new beauty: the beauty of speed. A racing car whose hood is adorned with great pipes, like serpents of explosive breath—a roaring car that seems to ride on grapeshot is more beautiful than the Victory of Samothrace.

5. We want to hymn the man at the wheel, who hurls the lance of his spirit across the Earth, along the circle of its orbit.

6. The poet must spend himself with ardour, splendour, and generosity, to swell the enthusiastic fervour of the primordial elements.

7. Except in struggle, there is no more beauty. No work without an aggressive character can be a masterpiece. Poetry must be conceived as a violent attack on unknown forces, to reduce and prostrate them before man.

8. We stand on the last promontory of the centuries!.... Why should we look back, when what we want is to break down the mysterious doors of the impossible? Time and space died yesterday. We already live in the absolute, because we have created eternal, omnipresent speed.

9. We will glorify war—the world's only hygiene—militarism, patriotism, the destructive gestures of freedom-bringers, beautiful ideas worth dying for, and scorn for women.

10. We will destroy the museums, libraries, academies of every kind, we will fight moralism, feminism, every opportunistic or utilitarian cowardice.

11. We will sing of great crowds excited by work, by pleasure and by riot; we will sing of the multi-colored polyphonic tide of revolution in the modern capitals; we will sing of the vibrant nightly fervor of arsenals and shipyards blazing with violent electric moons; greedy railway stations that devour smoke-plumed serpents; factories hung on clouds by the crooked lines of their smoke; bridges that stride the rivers like giant gymnasts, flashing in the sun with a glitter of knives; adventurous steamers that sniff the horizon; deep chested locomotives whose wheels paw the tracks like the hooves of enormous steel horses bridled by tubing; and the sleek flight of planes whose propellers chatter in the wind like banners and seem to cheer like an enthusiastic crowd.

It is from Italy that we launch through the world this violently upsetting incendiary manifesto of ours. With it, today, we establish Futurism, because we want to free this land from its smelly gangrene of professors, archaeologists, ciceroni and antiquarians. For too long has Italy been a dealer in second-hand clothes. We mean to free her from the numberless museums that cover her like so many graveyards.
   Museums; cemeteries!... Identical, surely, in the sinister promiscuity of so many bodies unknown to one another. Museums: public dormitories where one lies forever beside hated or unknown beings. Museums: absurd abatoirs of painters and sculptors ferociously slaughtering each other with color-blows and line-blows, the length of the fought-over walls!
   That one should make an annual pilgrimage, just as one goes to the graveyard on All Soul's Day—that I grant. That once a year one should leave a floral tribute beneath the Gioconda, I grant you that... But I don't admit that our sorrows, our fragile courage, our morbid restlessnes should be given a daily tour through the museums. Why poison ourselves? Why rot?
   And what is there to see in an old picture except the laborious contortions of an artist throwing himself against the barriers that thwart his desire to express his dream completely?... Admiring an old picture is the same as pouring our sensibility into a funerary urn instead of hurling it far off, in violent spasms of action and creation.
   Do you, then, wish to waste all your best powers in this eternal and futile worship of the past, from which you emerge fatally exhausted, shrunken, beaten down?
   In truth I tell you that daily visits to the museums, libraries and academies (cemeteries of empty exertion, Calvaries of crucified dreams, registries of aborted beginnings!) are, for artists, as damaging as the prolonged supervision by parents of certain young people drunk with their talent and their ambitious wills. When the future is barred to them, the admirable past may be a solace for the ills of the moribund,

the sickly, the prisoner... But we want no part of it, the past, we the young and strong Futurists!

So let them come, the gay incendiaries with charred fingers! Here they are! Here they are!... Come on! set fire to the library shelves! Turn aside the canals to flood the museums!... Oh, the joy of seeing the glorious old canvases bobbing adrift on these waters, discolored and shredded!.... Take up your pickaxes, your axes and hammers and wreck, wreck the venerable cities piteously!

The oldest of us is thirty: so we have at least a decade for finishing our work. When we are forty, other younger and stronger men will probably throw us in the waste-basket like useless manuscripts—We want it to happen!

They will come against us, our successors, will come from far away, from every quarter, dancing to the winged cadence of their first songs, flexing the hooked claws of predators, sniffing doglike at the academy doors the strong odor of our decaying minds, which will already have been promised to the literary catacombs.

But we won't be there... At last they'll find us—one winter's night—in open country, beneath a sad roof drummed by a monotonous rain. They'll see us crouched beside our trembling aeroplanes in the act of warming our hands at the poor little blaze that our books of today will give out when they take fire from the flight of our images.

They'll storm around us, panting with scorn and anguish, and all of them, exasperated by our proud daring, will hurtle to kill us, driven by a hatred the more implacable the more their hearts will be drunk with love and admiration for us.

Injustice, strong and sane, will break out radiantly in their eyes.

Art, in fact, can be nothing but violence, cruelty, and injustice.

The oldest of us is thirty: even so we have already scattered treasures, a thousand treasures of force, love, courage, astuteness, and raw willpower; have thrown them impatiently away, with fury, carelessly, unhesitatingly, breathless, and unresting... Look at us! We are still untired! Our hearts know no weariness because they are fed with fire, hatred, and speed!... Does that amaze you? It should, because you can never remember having lived! Erect on the summit of the world, once again we hurl our defiance to the stars!

You have objections? Enough! Enough! We know them... We've understood!... Our fine deceitful intelligence tells us that we are the revival and extension of our ancestors—Perhaps!... If only it were so! —But who cares? We don't want to understand!... Woe to anyone who says those infamous words to us again!

Lift up your heads!

Erect on the summit of the world, once again we hurl defiance to the stars.[8]

Historians and writers have attempted to discount Marinetti's political impact due to the relationship between Fascism and Futurism after 1917. Much that has been written about the movement separates some artists from their politics or dismisses the movement lightly. James Joll in his book, *The Intellectual in Politics,* argues that there was nothing essentially original in Marinetti's polemic and that he borrowed heavily from groups and ideas already widely held among various European intellectuals.

There was nothing new in all this. The admiration for destruction was common enough at a moment when Nietzsche's influence in France and Italy was at its height, and when Georges Sorel was elevating violence into a political doctrine. Indeed, a group of minor writers and artists, who had founded in Paris a group called Campagnons de L'action d'Art, based on a mixture of anarchist and Nietzschean ideas, had already gone so far as to publish a manifesto in 1907—two years before the Futurists—in which they proclaimed the necessity of resorting to violence to preserve the dignity of art, declared the inequality of man, and exclaimed 'Long live the violence against all that makes life ugly!' And, as many of Marinetti's contemporaries were pointing out, Walt Whitman, Zola, Verheeren and others had already been concerned to glorify 'Les villes tentaculaires'...[9] Moreover, at a higher intellectual level, Bergson had been teaching the importance of understanding the nature of speed and motion if we were to be able to evaluate and interpret our sensory perceptions of the world around us.[10]

Jane Raye in her work *Futurism* adopts the same deprecating attitude.

Many responded to Marinetti's rallying cry; others, in carping spirit, pointed out that there was nothing very new in all this, which was undoubtedly true. Belief in the power and virtue of youth had been strong in the Nineteenth Century, since the Romantic movement, and particularly so in Italy where Mazzini's Italian Youth had been such a powerful political force. Many writers, and to a lesser extent painters, had observed the beauty of machines and the artistic possibilities of the industrial age since Baudelaire had exhorted the artist to concern himself with 'the heroism of modern life.'[11]

However reassuring these arguments may sound to the politically naive that Marinetti's influence and impact were circumscribed and undermined by his lack of originality, the fact remains that very nearly single handed, F.T. Marinetti propelled Italy into the twentieth century and prepared her people in a way totally unprecedented for the holocaust of war and political upheaval. He did this so well that he sparked a national outcry to end passéism[12] and political compromise and he spearheaded the pressure groups which compelled the government to immediately begin a campaign of aggression against the Turkish-held city of Tripoli in 1911-12.

The influence and appeal of Marinetti's bellicose ideology spread throughout all classes of Italian society and found support in diverse political camps. Monarchists, Papists, revolutionaries, republicans and nationalists all found themselves in sympathy with the principle of Italian expansion, both into the Austrian-held provinces in the north and along the Mediterranean coast of Africa. Futurism, the name Marinetti gave the movement in 1909, was generally recognized as a major artistic and political force which instigated fundamental policy changes at upper echelons of government.[13]

The means the Futurists employed to effect these changes seem familiar and predictable after sixty years of similar "civil disorders." Meetings, riots, speeches, poetic tournaments, raucous theatricals, staged and unstaged assaults, picket lines, rallies, boycotts, and spectaculars of incredible variety erupted from one end of Italy to the other. Sometimes simultaneous disturbances occurred in several cities at once; more often Marinetti directed successive campaigns in one city after another, resting and refining his strategy on trains which carried him around the country at befitting break-neck speed. The style of the Futurists' campaign against passéism was as powerful an influence on public opinion as the content of their proliferous manifestos. The high visibility of the movement penetrated the most obscure areas of Italian life, urban and provincial. Factory walls, dance halls, theatres, cafés and public squares were overlaid with Futurist posters, while newspapers and journals carried detailed accounts of both political and artistic activities. For Marinetti was, above all, a master salesman, a baron of the flourishing empire of advertising, who capitalized on every notoriety gaining device available in the new technological age.

Ultimately all the energy of the Futurists was directed towards accomplishing the African Campaign, which was undertaken in 1911. This colonizing effort was an important event in assessing the widespread acceptance of militarism in Italy, which had become Marinetti's special prerogative. Although badly managed from a military point of view,[14] the Italian campaign succeeded in acquiring Tripoli, Libya and the Dodecanese Islands in the treaty of 1912. Not only did this treaty signify the collapse of the Ottoman Empire, but it also indicated the newly substantiated bargaining power which Italy had been seeking among the European and Eastern powers. This accomplishment satisfied, for the moment, Italy's desire to participate in colonial expansion. In addition, Italy had concluded treaties with France which allowed full and free citizenship for Italians in Tunis, a problem which had impeded the improvement of Franco-Italian relations. Moreover, the Tripolitan expedition set the new tenor of Italian foreign policy and Italy's ambitions were now recognized throughout Europe.

Soon after the conclusion of the Tripolitan Treaty, Italian interest shifted away from the Triple Alliance (Germany, Austria-Hungary, and Italy) toward an alliance with France and England, and the Entente Cordiale. Marinetti was particularly active in establishing a foundation for a French-Italian alliance which he considered of paramount importance for political and artistic reasons. Marinetti and those who followed him had so significantly impressed the Futurist position into international affairs that, in 1911, Camille Mauclair wrote in "Dêpeche de Toulouse," under the heading "Futurism and Young Italy":

> It cannot be denied that in the recent Tripolitan exploit, Italy has evinced qualities of pride, of contemptuous disregard for legality, and of lyrical aggressiveness which are but confirmations of the boastful arrogance of the Futurists. This is the reason why Futurism, sprung from literary paradoxes, deserves to be taken into consideration. Whether we like it or not it has already established itself as something that must be reckoned with in dealing with Italy. Many of their compatriots will

join the Futurists, won over by their passionate patriotism. War for the conquest of Trent and the control of the Adriatic is their dream.

Marinetti with characteristic vociferousness made the utmost of his moment of glory. In a speech to Italian Tripoli in 1912 he said:

> We Futurists who for the last two years, amidst the loud protests of our gouty and paralytic compatriots, have been proclaiming the beauty of danger and of violence, extolling the love of country and of war, preaching strife as the cure for all the world's ailments, are now happy to see Italy triumphant and the unholy brood of pacifists passing away in the dungeons of the ridiculous Palace of the Hague.
>
> Having recently, and with much satisfaction, punched the faces of all those who tried with their frantic shrieks to prevent a declaration of war, we now proclaim against all pacifists the following principles:
>
> 1. All liberties shall be granted except the right to be a coward.
>
> 2. Let it be understood that the word Italy tops the word liberty.
>
> 3. The loathsome memory of Roman greatness must vanish in the splendor of infinitely greater Italian victories.[15]

The "infinitely greater Italian victories" which Marinetti had in mind were the reacquisition of the Austrian-held provinces of Trentino and Istria, the former bordering the Brenner Pass in the north and the latter located on the Adriatic. This policy was called irredentist and had been a rallying cry for Northern Italians since the seventeenth century. These two provinces weighed heavily upon the national consciousness of many Italians. Italian-speaking students in these provinces had been badly treated by Austrian police during riots which had become more brutal and frequent in the preceeding ten years. Italian farmers and shopkeepers paid unequal taxes and suffered financial discrimination so that generally there was much rancor between the two "allies" over the question of government in those areas. In fact, the idea of completing the unification of Italy begun in the 1860's was a coalescing force in a politically fragmented country. For despite growing popular cognizance of an Italian national interest with a centralized parliamentary government, many factions, especially the Socialists and Catholics, were still sporadic in their support of the government. The Socialists, for example, were outraged by the African Campaign and by all nationalistic platforms which advocated military activities for further annexation or colonization no matter what claims Italy might produce.[16]

Marinetti took up the Austrian problem with his celebrated vigor. He had already been arrested in Trieste in 1908 for participating in a funeral demonstration for the mother of an executed Italian revolutionary.[17] Joll says of

Marinetti during these years: "He had many qualities that fitted him to be a leader of a new movement—a quick, eclectic, superficial intelligence, leisure, money, considerable personal charm, optimism and, above all, boundless energy."[18] Now, with the mood ripe for Italian intervention against the Austrian-held territories, Marinetti conducted an effective and colorful campaign to rally support for the acquisition of the northern provinces, either by negotiation or by armed force. In 1911 Marinetti wrote in an essay published in Turin:

> Ah, when will we finally invent masks and coveralls to protect ourselves from the deadly infection of imbecility, the imbecility that you betray, you who naturally dislike the cruel sincerity of my attacks on Italian passéism? You say that everyone should wash his own dirty laundry in private... Nonsense! We are no subtle and delicate-handed washerwomen. Today we make joyful bonfire of our infected, pestilential laundry on the loftiest peak of human thought.
>
> We spare no one. After having insulted every stranger who adores our Italian past and despises us as singers of serenades, as ciceroni or beggars, we have asked them to admire us as the most gifted race on earth.
>
> Thanks to us, Italy will cease to be the loveroom of the cosmopolitan world.
>
> To this end we have undertaken to propagandize courage against the epidemic of cowardice, to create an artificial optimism against chronic pessimism. Our hatred of Austria; our feverish anticipation of war; our desire to strangle Pan-Germanism. This is the corollary of our Futurist theorem!... Then silence, imbeciles! We hurl ourselves against you, holding our hearts in our fingers like revolvers, our hearts burdened with hate and courage.[19]

Again Marinetti resorted to the most efficacious means for propagandizing his position. Giovanni Papini, a long time literary adversary, who had been finally won over to the Futurist camp, described Marinetti's tactics in the prewar period of 1913-15.

> His arrival in the peaceful city of Florence of those days was like a meteorite landing in an old palace garden. Telegrams, telephone calls, rides in motor cars, appointments made and put off, tumultuous dinner parties, mass invasions of respectable cafés. He was always rushing from one place to another, writing, orating, organizing.[20]

His efforts were finally rewarded not by an armed action against Austria but by the erosion of Italy's alliance with Germany and Austro-Hungary, which resulted in a period of neutrality, a policy of "wait and see" as Europe rolled inevitably towards war. Finally, in 1915 Italy negotiated the Pact of London which granted Italy the Trentino, Cisalpine Tyrol, Istria, Trieste, most of Dalmatia and a number of islands in the Adriatic, but explicitly excluded the city of Fiume on the Istrian border of Yugoslavia. Agreements were also concluded which granted Italy compensation from the partition of Germany's

Regions of Italy with World War I Acquisitions

African colonies and a share in the eventual partition of the Ottoman Empire. In exchange, Italy guaranteed to come into the war, not as a member of the Triple Alliance, but on the side of France, England and Russia. Italy met her commitment by declaring war on Austria alone in May 1915. She did not expand her war declaration to include Germany until August 1916. In the intervening fifteen months a series of internal crises occurred between the Italian parliament and the King's chief ministers. In fact, the vast majority of the Italian population was absolutely neutralist, a position which was quite tenable to the various hostile parties who would rather have had Italy stay out of the war altogether than come in on the "wrong side." No other country in Europe up to 1915 had so completely disguised her intentions as had Italy through years of the most delicately ambiguous political acts. However, the carefully wrought shield of neutrality and non-intervention, like so much that had been attacked as passéist, was finally penetrated by the small minority of Nationalists, interventionalists, reform socialists, irredentists, republicans, Freemasons, radicals and anti-German liberals whose only platform for coalition was their mutual desire to push Italy into the war. With celebrations that continued on into and even after the holocaust of the Great War, the Futurists realized their principle political aim, that Italy might affirm her entrance into the modern world by the act of "War, the World's Only Hygiene,"[21] the ultimate statement of the supremacy of electric energy, speed, technology, science and destruction. "In war," the Futurists reasoned, "the past glory can be finally muted, the museums and libraries burnt, and a greater stronger, more astonishing Italy will rise from the rubble. . ."[22] They went into the front lines; many did not survive the rejuvenating hygiene of the Great War and died in fine Futurist manner upon the battlefield.

Futurism's role in undermining the influence of liberal-moderate government in Italy and therefore of laying the foundation upon which Fascism was to be built after the end of the war in 1919 should be apparent from this short political history. Once the main lines of Futurist propaganda have been understood, what is interesting about Marinetti's activities in these years is the way in which he conducted his campaign to stir up public opinion. By stopping at nothing, by using all the devices of publicity he could invent, by revelling in noise, fights and opposition, he forced the public to listen to his slogans, a good many of which stuck in their minds. As Benedetto Croce wrote in 1924:

> For anyone who has a sense of historical connections, the ideological origins of Fascism can be found in Futurism, in the determination to go down into the streets, to impose their own opinion, to stop the mouths of those who disagree, not to fear riots or fights, in this eagerness to break with all traditions, in this exaltation of youth which was characteristic of Futurism. . .[23]

This was a harsh judgment, not altogether true, but written in a spirit of despair and hatred by the aging philosopher-historian whose life work was being destroyed by Mussolini's tyranny. Moreover, it is true that Marinetti was utterly manipulated by the Fascists, promoted, used and finally discarded when the complete machinery of their ideology took hold of the country. Suffice it to say that Futurism was a sizeable factor in the politics of Italy from 1909 to 1920, and that the methodology so cleverly employed by Marinetti and his followers had a decisive impact on the history of Italy, Europe and the world in the years to come. The entire movement, political and artistic, had been so consistently identified with Fascism that research and publicity which has attempted to analyze and describe the activities of the Futurists has been greatly suppressed in Italy until fairly recently. Obviously this has made the work of reclaiming documents, pictures, and letters more difficult. Happily, the current of public and academic opinion has shifted and Futurism is now regarded as an important and interesting manifestation of political art in itself and apart from its connection with Fascism.

It is not the intention of this work to deal with Fascism but rather at this juncture to examine the other half of the movement, Futurist art, most especially the art of Futurist performance which has played a large role in Futurist politics in the form of staged and unstaged spectacles, riots, meetings, and in a type of formal theatre pieces unique to the movement. For, whereas the ramifications of Futurist political ideology rightly belong to the area of political history, the impact of Futurism on the greater part of the twentieth century art will be shown to be very much a factor in the development of theatre history. Moreover, the legacy of the Futurists which has passed to such groups as the Dadaists, Surrealists, Absurdists, practitioners of Happenings, Events and Assembleges, and to the vast panoply of agit-prop theatre companies throughout the western world confirms one of the hypotheses of this study: that the Futurists, by the most inventive and imaginative means, had an impact on artistic ideology which cannot be ignored and which even today is not wholly exhausted.

II

PAINTING

After the publication of the "Foundation Manifesto" in 1909, Marinetti became the leader of a movement which was determined to produce more than a rebellion against syntax and rhymed verse and the political status quo, a movement which would penetrate and redefine activities and aesthetics in the fields of painting, sculpture, music, photography, architecture and theatre. In short, Marinetti very quickly became the central figure in a revolution in the arts, a revolution which was inextricably bound to his political ideology as described in the previous section of this work.

Marinetti's politics were essentially doctrinaire and were ultimately subjected to manipulation by the Fascists. His views concerning the reconstruction of standards and values in the arts, however, were decidedly more pragmatic, the result of vigorous collaboration between himself and the artists who were gathering around him. The result of this collaboration was the production of systematic, radical manifestos which attempted to reconcile the arts with the technological age. This reconciliation was predicated upon disassociating the arts from the entire development of art since pre-history.

The tone and philosophy of the manifestos regarding painting, sculpture, architecture, music and theatre echo the tone and philosophy found in the "Foundation Manifesto," although many of these succeeding documents were not written by Marinetti. So powerful was the force of his personality and the style of his prose that it permeated even the technical descriptions produced by other Futurist artists.

The first manifesto to describe a Futurist theory of art was the "Painter's Manifesto" of March 1910,[1] written primarily by Umberto Boccioni with input from the Futurist painters Carlo Carrà, Luigi Russolo, Giacomo Balla and Gino Severini.

Manifesto of the Futurist Painters 1910
Boccioni, Carrà, Russolo, Balla, Severini
published by *Poesia* 11 Feb. 1910

To the young artists of Italy!
The cry of rebellion which we utter associates our ideals with those of the Futurist poets. These ideals were not invented by some aesthetic clique. They are the expression of a violent desire which boils in the veins of every creative artist today.

We will fight with all our might the fanatical, senseless and snobbish religion of the past, a religion encouraged by the vicious existence of museums. We rebel against that spineless worshipping of old canvases, old statues and old bric-a-brac, against everything which is filthy and worm-ridden and corroded by time. We consider

15

the habitual contempt for everything which is young, new and burning with life to be unjust and even criminal.

Comrades, we tell you now that that triumphant progress of science makes profound changes in humanity inevitable, changes which are hacking an abyss between those docile slaves of past tradition and us free moderns, who are confident in the radiant splendour of our future.

We are sickened by the foul laziness of artists who, ever since the sixteenth century, have endlessly exploited the glories of the ancient Romans.

In the eyes of other countries, Italy is still a land of the dead, a vast Pompeii, white with sepulchres. But Italy is being reborn, its political resurgence will be followed by a cultural resurgence. In the land inhabited by the illiterate peasant, schools will be set up; in the land where doing nothing in the sun was the only available profession, millions of machines are already roaring; in the land where traditional aesthetics reigned supreme, new flights of artistic inspiration are emerging and dazzling the world with their brilliance.

Living art draws its life from the surrounding environment. Our forebears drew their artistic inspiration from a religious atmosphere which fed their souls; in the same way we must breathe in the tangible miracles of a contemporary life—the iron network of speedy communications which envelops the earth, the transatlantic liners, the dreadnoughts, those marvellous flights which furrow our skies, the profound courage of our submarine navigators and the spasmodic struggle to conquer the unknown. How can we remain insensible to the frenetic life of our great cities and to the exciting new psychology of night-life; the feverish figures of the bon viveur, the coquette, the apache and the absinthe drinker?

We will also play our part in this crucial revivial of aesthetic expression; we declare war on all artists and all institutions which insist on hiding behind a facade of false modernity, while they are actually ensnared by tradition, academicism and, above all, a nauseating cerebral laziness.

We condemn as insulting to youth the acclamations of a revolting rabble for the sickening reflowering of a pathetic kind of classicism in Rome; the neurasthenic cultivation of hermaphroditic archaism which they rave about in Florence; the pedestrian, half-blind handiwork of '48 which they are buying in Milan, the work of pensioned-off government clerks which they think the world of in Turin; the hotchpotch of encrusted rubbish of a group of fossilized alchemists which they are worshipping in Venice. We are going to rise up against all superficiality and banality—all the slovenly and facile commercialism which makes the work of most of our highly respected artists throughout Italy worthy of our deepest contempt.

Away then with hired restorers of antiquated incrustations. Away with affected archaeologists with their chronic necrophilia! Down with the critics, those complacent pimps! Down with the gouty academics and drunken, ignorant professors!

Ask these priests of a veritable religious cult, these guardians of old aesthetic laws, where we can go and see the works of Giovanni Segantini today. Ask them why the officials of the Commission have never heard of the existence of Gaetano Previati. Ask them where they can see Medardo Rosso's sculpture, or who takes the slightest interest in artists who have not yet had twenty years of struggle and suffering behind them, but are still producing works destined to honor their fatherland?

These paid critics have other interests to defend. Exhibitions, competitions, superficial and never disinterested criticism, condemn Italian art to the ignominy of true prostitution.

And what about our esteemed 'specialists'? Throw them all out. Finish them off! The Portraitists, the Genre Painters, the Lake Painters, the Mountain Painters. We have put up with enough from these impotent painters of country holidays.

Down with the marble-chippers who are cluttering up our squares and profaning our cemeteries! Down with the speculators and their reinforced-concrete buildings! Down with the laborious decorators, phony ceramicists, sold-out poster painters and shoddy, idiotic illustrators!

These are our final conclusions:

With our enthusiastic adherence to Futurism, we will:

1. Destroy the cult of the past, the obsession with the ancients, pedantry and academic formalism.
2. Totally invalidate all kinds of imitation.
3. Elevate all attempts at originality, however daring, however violent.
4. Bear bravely and proudly the smear of 'madness' with which they try to gag all innovators.
5. Regard art critics as useless and dangerous.
6. Rebel against the tyranny of words: "Harmony" and "good taste" and other loose expressions which can be used to destroy the works of Rembrandt, Goya, Rodin...
7. Sweep the whole field of art clean of all themes and subjects which have been used in the past.
8. Support and glory in our day-to-day world, a world which is going to be continually and splendidly transformed by victorious Science.

The dead shall be buried in the earth's deepest bowels! The threshold of the future will be swept free of mummies! Make room for youth, for violence, for daring![2]

The "Manifesto of the Futurist Painters" was the first publication to deal with the translation of Marinetti's "Foundation Manifesto" concepts into a specific art form. Heavily influenced by the style of Marinetti's document, the "Painter's Manifesto" attacks the many obstacles to the Futurist campaign which stand between the artists of the new movement and their soon to be enlightened public. The Manifesto does not describe the specific nature of the new Futurist art in visual terms, nor does it instruct the Futurist painter in his struggle to develop a pictorial representation which would "Support and glory in our day to day world, a world which is going to be continually and splendidly transformed by victorious Science." The Manifesto does begin to select the new vocabulary, the iron network of speedy communication, transatlantic liners, dreadnoughts, airplanes, and city life. What the painters advocated in 1910 was a renovation in public attitude which had traditionally looked to the past and supported the most reactionary tendencies in art.

By the end of the year 1910, the Futurist painters had begun to establish the vocabulary and style of painting which was to compliment and support the demands of the new movement until the war in 1915. Throughout 1910 and 1911, a dozen or so Futurist painters worked to refine and improve their new techniques which they exhibited to the world in Paris at the Galerie Bernheim-Jeune in February 1912. The importance of this first internationally publicized show of Futurist art was noted by the leading critics, including Apollinaire. The show left the Bernheim-Jeune for a six month tour which included London, Berlin and Moscow. In the catalogue of the exhibition the Futurists Carrà, Boccioni, Russolo, Balla and Severini defined their intentions and explicated the important technical innovations which they had developed. Their message, called "Exhibitors to the Public," was a manifesto of great importance.

We may declare, without boasting, that the first Exhibition of Italian Futurist Painting, recently held in Paris and now brought to London, is the most important exhibition of Italian painting which has hitherto been offered to the judgment of Europe.

For we are young and our art is violently revolutionary.

What we have attempted and accomplished, while attracting around us a large number of skilful imitators and as many plagiarists without talent, has placed us at the head of the European movement in painting, by a road different from, yet, in a way, parallel with, that followed by the Post-impressionists, Synthetists and Cubists of France, led by their masters Picasso, Braque, Derain, Metzinger, Le Fauconnier, Gleizes, Léger, Lhote, etc.

While we admire the heroism of these painters of great worth, who have displayed a laudable contempt for artistic commercialism and a powerful hatred of academism, we feel ourselves and we declare ourselves to be absolutely opposed to their art.

They obstinately continue to paint objects motionless, frozen, and all the static aspects of Nature; they worship the traditionalism of Poussin, of Ingres, of Corot, ageing and petrifying their art with an obstinate attachment to the past, which to our eyes remains totally incomprehensible.

We, on the contrary, with points of view pertaining essentially to the future, seek for a style of motion, a thing which has never been attempted before us.

Far from resting upon the examples of the Greeks and the Old Masters, we constantly extol individual intuition; our object is to determine completely new laws which may deliver painting from the wavering uncertainty in which it lingers.

Our desire, to give as far as possible to our pictures a solid construction, can never bear us back to any tradition whatsoever. Of that we are firmly convinced.

All the truths learnt in the schools or in the studios are abolished for us. Our hands are free enough and pure enough to start everything afresh.

Is it indisputable that several of the aesthetic declarations of our French comrades display a sort of masked academism.

Is it not, indeed a return to the Academy to declare that the subject, in painting, is of perfectly insignificant value?

We declare, on the contrary, that there can be no modern painting without the starting point of an absolutely modern sensation, and none can contradict us when we state that *painting* and *sensation* are two inseparable words.

If our pictures are Futurist, it is because they are the result of absolutely Futurist conceptions, ethical, aesthetic, political, social.

To paint from the posing model is an absurdity, and an act of mental cowardice, even if the model be translated upon the picture in linear, spherical or cubic forms.

To lend an allegorical significance to an ordinary nude figure, deriving the meaning of the picture from the objects held by the model or from those which are arranged about him, is to our mind the evidence of a traditional and academic mentality.

This method, very similar to that employed by the Greeks, by Raphael, by Titian, by Veronese, must necessarily displease us.

While we repudiate Impressionism, we emphatically condemn the present reaction which, in order to kill Impressionism, brings back painting to old academic forms.

It is only possible to react against Impressionism by surpassing it.

Nothing is more absurd than to fight it by adopting the pictural laws which preceded it.

The points of contact which the quest of style may have with the so-called *classic art* do not concern us.

Others will seek, and will, no doubt, discover these analogies which in any case cannot be looked upon as a return to methods, conceptions and values transmitted by classical painting.

A few examples will illustrate our theory.

We see no difference between one of those nude figures commonly called artistic and an anatomical plate. There is, on the other hand, an enormous difference between one of these nude figures and our Futurist conception of the human body.

Perspective, such as it is understood by the majority of painters, has for us the same value which they lend to an engineer's design.

simultaneousness of states of mind in the work of art: that is the intoxi-
of our art.

explain again by examples. In painting a person on a balcony, seen from
om, we do not limit the scene to what the square frame of the window
e; but we try to render the sum total of visual sensations which the
balcony has experienced; the sun-bathed throng in the street, the
houses which stretch to right and left, the beflowered balconies, etc.
he simultaneousness of the ambient, and, therefore, the dislocation
ment of objects, the scattering and fusion of details, freed from
nd independent from one another.

make the spectator live in the centre of the picture, as we express it
of *who*, the picture must be the synthesis of *what one remembers* and
You

what wder the invisible which stirs and lives beyond intervening obstacles,
square of the right, on the left, and behind us, and not merely the small
We ha cially compressed, as it were, by the wings of a stage.
sensation, ed in our manifesto that what must be rendered is the *dynamic
movement*, o say, the particular rhythm of each object, its inclination, its
It is usua exactly, its interior force.
stillness, or joy nsider the human being in its different aspects of motion or
What is over citement or grave melancholy.
frenzy, sadness d is that all inanimate objects display, by their lines, calmness or
are formed a sense iety. These various tendencies lend to the lines of which they
character of weighty stability or of aerial lightness.

Every object reveals by its lines how it would resolve itself were it to follow the tendencies of its forces.

This decomposition is not governed by fixed laws but it varies according to the characteristic personality of the object and the emotions of the onlooker.

Furthermore, every object influences its neighbour, not by reflections of light (the foundation of *Impressionistic primitivism*), but by a real competition of lines and by real conflicts of planes, following the emotional law which governs the picture (the foundation of *Futurist primitivism*).

With the desire to intensify the aesthetic emotions by blending, so to speak, the painted canvas with the soul of the spectator, we have declared that the latter *must in future be placed in the centre of the picture.*

He shall not be present at, but participate in the action. If we paint the phases of a riot, the crowd bustling with uplifted fists and the noisy onslaughts of cavalry are translated upon the canvas in sheaves of lines corresponding with all the conflicting forces, following the general law of violence of the picture.

These *force-lines* must encircle and involve the spectator so that he will in a manner be forced to struggle himself with the persons in the picture.

All objects, in accordance with what the painter Boccioni happily terms *physical transcendentalism,* tend to the infinite by their *force-lines,* the continuity of which is measured by our intuition.

It is these *force-lines* that we must draw in order to lead back the work of art to true painting. We interpret nature by rendering these objects upon the canvas as the beginnings or the prolongations of the rhythms impressed upon our sensibility by these very objects.

After having, for instance, reproduced in a picture the right shoulder or the right ear of a figure, we deem it totally vain and useless to reproduce the left shoulder or the left ear. We do not draw sounds, but their vibrating intervals. We do not draw diseases, but their symptoms and their consequences.

We may further explain our idea by a comparison drawn from the art of music.

Not only have we radically abandoned the motive fully developed with its determined, and, therefore, artificial equilibrium, but we suddenly intersect each motive with one or more other motives of which we never give the full development but merely the initial, central, or final notes.

As you see, there is with us not merely variety, but chaos and clashing rhythms, totally opposed to one another, which we nevertheless assemble into a new harmony.

We thus arrive at what we call the *painting of states of mind.*

In the pictural description of the various states of mind of a leave-taking, perpendicular lines, undulating and as it were worn out, clinging here and there to silhouettes of empty bodies, may well express languidness and discouragement.

Confused, and trepidating lines, either straight or curved, mingled with the outlined hurried gestures of people calling one another, will give a sensation of chaotic excitement.

On the other hand, horizontal lines, fleeting, rapid and brutally cutting into half lost profiles or faces or crumbling and rebounding fragments of landscape, will give the tumultuous feelings of the persons going away.

It is practically impossible to express in words the essential values of painting.

The public must also be convinced that in order to understand aesthetic sensations to which one is not accustomed, it is necessary to forget entirely one's intellectual culture, not in order to *assimilate* the work of art, but to *deliver one's self up* to it heart and soul.

We are beginning a new epoch of painting.

We are sure henceforward of realizing conceptions of the highest importance and the most unquestionable originality. Others will follow who, with equal daring and determination, will conquer those summits of which we can only catch a glimpse. That is why we have proclaimed ourselves to be the *primitives of a completely renovated sensitiveness*. In several of the pictures which we are presenting to the public, vibration and motion endlessly multiply each object. We have thus justified our famous statement regarding the *running horse which has not four legs, but twenty*.

One may remark, also, in our pictures spots, lines, zones of colour which do not correspond to any reality, but which, in accordance with a law of our interior mathematics, musically prepare and enhance the emotion of the spectator.

We thus create a sort of emotive ambience, seeking by intuition the sympathies and the links which exist between the exterior (concrete) scene and the interior (abstract) emotion. Those lines, those spots, those zones of colour, apparently illogical and meaningless, are the mysterious keys to our pictures.

We shall no doubt be taxed with an excessive desire to define and express in tangible form the subtle ties which unite our abstract interior with the concrete exterior.

Yet, could we leave an unfettered liberty of understanding to the public which always sees, as it has been taught to see, through eyes warped by routine?

We go our way, destroying each in ourselves and in our pictures the realistic forms and the obvious details which have served us to construct a bridge of understanding between ourselves and the public. In order that the crowd may enjoy our marvellous spiritual world, of which it is ignorant, we give it the material sensation of that world.

We thus reply to the coarse and simplistic curiosity which surrounds us by the brutally realistic aspects of our primitivism.

Conclusion: Our Futurist painting embodies three new conceptions of painting:

1. That which solves the question of volumes in a picture, as opposed to the liquefaction of objects favoured by the vision of the Impressionists.

2. That which leads us to translate objects according to the *force-lines* which distinguish them, and by which is obtained an absolutely new power of objective poetry.

3. That (the natural consequence of the other two) which would give the emotional ambience of a picture, the synthesis of the various abstract rhythms of every object, from which there springs a fount of pictural lyricism hitherto unknown.[3]

The concepts which the Futurist painters articulated in the "Exhibitors to the Public Manifesto" were seminal to the development of the visual movement and to every manifestation of Futurism. Not only were the goals of Futurist painting most influential in the articulation of goals for other Futurist media, but the techniques and methods of accomplishing these goals were vigorously translated into appropriate techniques and methodologies applicable to Futurist photography, architecture, music, literature, cinema, and theatre art.

The primary goal of Futurist painting was to transport the spectator to the center of the canvas, to involve him in the action of the painting and thus to awaken in him a resonance with the painter's vision, a vision of the "Inner Core of Being."[4] The spectator, drawn into the center of the painting by technical innovations, then becomes a participant in the action of the painting and shares sensitivities with the artist. This was a fundamentally Futurist concept, one which was a significant departure from the concepts of other artists. The Futurists focused attention on the activity of the spectator and on the possibilities which joint participation between the artist and viewer afforded the viewer. The Futurists rejected the passive stationary position of the spectator viewing the canvas from without and embraced an ideal wherein the spectator could interact with the artist's soul at the most profound level.

The "Exhibitors to the Public Manifesto" described in technical terms the method which would produce the desired response from the spectator and which would fully support Futurist aspirations to a completely modern style of painting. Their method was based upon the articulation and depiction of what they believed to be two states of movement. They called these two states of movement "dynamism." One state of dynamism was that which actually occurred and could be measured. They used the term "movement" to define any displacement of a whole object through space either in actuality or as it might occur in a Futurist painting where objects were pictured as though they were moving. The other state of dynamism, "motion," referred to the activity inherent in any substance or object which has mass and volume. The Futurists claimed to sense molecular movement and to see in their imaginations the atomic motion which philosophy suspected and science demonstrated. The capacity for sensing dynamism they called the dynamic sensation, a psychological ability for intuiting dynamism in what appeared to be static objects (motion) and in objects which were displaced through space (movement). To transport the spectator to the center of the painting and involve him in the painting it was necessary to instill in him this capacity for dynamic sensation. The Futurists assumed that the spectator could learn how to be dynamically sensitive from studying Futurist painting.

> The public must also be convinced that in order to understand aesthetic sensations to which one is not accustomed, it is necessary to forget entirely one's intellectual culture, not in order to assimilate the work of art, but to deliver one's self up to it heart and soul.[5]

The Futurists insisted that painting deal with dynamism. "Cosmic dynamism took hold of the Futurists' imagination like an inspiring demon and subjugated it to its power. In this state of poetic furor the artist tore from the object the concealing envelope, the outer form, and sank deep within, until he came in contact with those dynamic waves which constitute the object's inner reality."[6] It was this image revealed to the artist by "penetrating inspiration and dynamic sensitiveness"[7] that he strove to express pictorially.

In order to transfer this "dynamic inner reality of the object" to the canvas, the Futurist painters constructed a new syntax with the available vocabulary of forms. They began this construction with several observations concerned with the properties of dynamism, motion and movement. Perceiving motion in objects led to their perception of the modifications which occurred between neighboring objects. These modifications occurred through "chromatic reverberations and reciprocal color influences and also through actual emanations of masses."[8] This perception led them beyond the light-centered treatment of contrasting and complementary color science which had been explored by the Divisionists to a statement of the "interpenetrability of material."[9]

> Who can believe in the opacity of bodies, since our sharpened and multiplied sensitiveness has already penetrated the obscure manifestations of the medium? Why should we forget in our creations the doubled power of sight, capable of giving results analogous to those of the x-rays?[10]

The Futurist painters saw the reverberations and emanations of masses as competitive and conflicting lines and planes, rather than as manifestations of reflected light.

Another Futurist observation of the properties of dynamism led to a recognition among Futurist painters of the importance of the surrounding milieu of any subject matter. The surrounding milieu was made up of the internal vibrations of objects and the reverberations intuited between objects. The milieu also included "what one remembers and what one sees."[11] The Futurists contended that objects could only be apprehended in terms of their surroundings and that any milieu was the sum of the emanations of its various concrete components and the memory of previous emanations from objects no longer perceived.

These emanations and reverberations, present at the same time in the same place, produced for the Futurists the phenomenon they called simultaneity. Simultaneity occurred in the instance of interpenetrating reverberations and emanations between objects and through objects. Simultaneity occurred whenever dynamism occurred in that dynamism implied several activities or actions occurring at the same time. However, the most useful application of the principle of simultaneity was in describing the qualities of an environment or a state of mind. The principle of simultaneity explained the concurrent existence of various physical and psychological conditions.

> In painting a person on a balcony, seen from inside the room, we do not limit the scene to what the square frame of the window renders visible; but we try to

render the sum total of visual sensations which the person on the balcony has experienced; the sunbathed throng in the street, the double row of houses which stretch to right and left, the beflowered balconies, etc. This implies the simultaneousness of the ambient, and, therefore, the dislocation and dismemberment of objects, the scattering and fusion of details, freed from accepted logic, and independent from one another.[12]

Simultaneity was also described by Ardengo Soffici, a well established art critic who joined the Futurists in 1912. The following explanation appeared in the press following a lecture held at the Verdi Theatre in Florence in 1913.[13]

> We Futurists claim that a pictorial synthesis may be inspired, not alone by the aspects of reality within the field of vision of one who looks at a natural motif, but by all aspects near or far, in time or in space, which seem valuable as elements of a suggestive integration. What appears to the man in the street as a panoramic view made by pasting picture cards together, is to the artistic eye the expression of a very broad zone of emotional life reflected and plastically concentrated in a very limited space.

Force-lines were the device which the Futurists invented to express the properties of dynamism—interpenetrability of material, a surrounding ambient, and simultaneity—in pictorial terms. Force-lines were explained as the dissolving perimeters of objects a they emanated outwards through the environment. These moving perimeters then met other moving perimeters from other objects in the environment and were resolved according to the characteristic 'personality' of the objects.

> What is overlooked is that all inanimate objects display, by their lines, calmness or frenzy, sadness or gaiety. These various tendencies lend to the lines of which they are formed a sense of character of weighty stability or of aerial lightness.
> Every object reveals by its lines how it would resolve itself were it to follow the tendencies of its forces.[14]

Some objects were seen by the Futurists as having soft surfaces or contours, while others were hard and resistant. Consequently, at any point where the force-lines of one object encountered the force-lines of another object they were both modified by that point of contact, and one field of force-lines was (generally) depicted as being more solid or more energized than the other group of force-lines.

Force-lines were also used as a Futurist device to transpose the spectator from the outside to the center of the painting. The Futurist painter used force-lines to indicate where his construction ended and the intuition of the spectator should begin to operate. "A force-line was a direction of color-force which was representative of the movements of matter along a trajectory determined by the structure of the object and its action."[15] Force-lines were the continuation of the rhythms which the object imprinted on the artist's mind. By conveying object-dynamism on the canvas the artist enabled the spectator to perceive the emanations, and in this way he was learning to perceive dynamism in the way prescribed by the Futurists and at the same time entering (through his participation) into the painting. Once the spectator apprehended the process of "dynamic sensitiveness" he was then able to continue to see the action of the painted objects and their force-lines moving off the canvas into the actual environment. That is, the action of the canvas moved out from the objects in the form of force-lines, thereby creating an illusion of motion and movement around the spectator. Consequently, the Futurists called this process the transferring of the spectator into the center of the canvas. This was an essential accomplishment to the Futurists, for it was through the transfer of the spectator to the center of the pictorial action that the spectator could experience dynamic sensations and become "one with the central core of things"[16] as the artist had done.

Soffici, writing in *Lacerba,* explained that the Futurist did not paint as though he were looking on from the outside, and gradually making his way to the inner core of life, but rather as though he were living at the center of things and expressing in color and line his participation in this inner life.[17] Boccioni described the process in *Pittuera scultara futurist.*

> In order that the spectator live at the center of a painted action, the tableau must be a synthesis not only of what we see, but also of what we recall (simultaneity). We must paint the invisible which stirs and lives beyond walls and barriers, which is on our right, on our left, and behind us . . .[18]

Carlo Carrà, writing in *Poesia,* said:

> We Futurists strive, with the power of our intuition, to identify ourselves with the central core of things so that our ego, on beholding them in their uniqueness, becomes one with them. We use plastic surfaces to express spherical emanations in space, and thus we obtain that sense of the perpetually mobile which is characteristic of all life. . .[19]

These concepts—dynamism, simultaneity, transposition of the spectator, force-lines, penetration of materiality, importance of surrounding environment— were the central theses of the painters' manifestos between 1910 and 1917. Clearly these concepts originated in the ideas expressed by Marinetti in the "Foundation Manifesto" of 1909, although the researches and experiments of earlier painters were also reflected in the theories of the Futurist painters. However, the innovations proffered by the Futurists were in no way less important because of their antecedents; on the contrary, it was their clarity of direction and the originality of their techniques which separated them from other groups of painters whose stylistic identity remained vague.

Futurist painters were exceptional in their ability to create a market for their work. The education of the art collector or spectator was twofold: first, to bombard him with manifestos and explanations of manifestos and then to surround him with Futurist canvases. This process was successful, despite large quantities of adverse criticism, both in and out of Italy. The London show of Futurist painting in 1912 was completely sold out, as was the Berlin Show of 1913. Even in Paris, traditionally hostile to innovations from outside France, most of the paintings were sold, possibly due to the publicity generated by the feud in the press between Apollinaire and the Futurists.[20] The principles contained in their documents and the effect of Futurist paintings caused an artistic and emotional furor wherever they were presented. Gallery shows became battlegrounds both metaphorically and in actuality as the painters heartily embraced the Futurist philosophy of violent confrontation, provocation and belligerence in the face of any opposition to the movement. Carlo Carrà recalled the first reading of the "Painter's Manifesto" at the Chiarella Theatre in Turin in 1910, "We exchanged as many hits as ideas"[21] as well as shouts, whistles, over-ripe fruit and rancid spaghetti, but this was to become the "grand tradition of Futurism" and, according to Marinetti, was the supreme indication of Futurist success. Marinetti described the "grand Futurist tradition" in these words:

> We teach. . . the pleasure of being booed. Not everything booed is beautiful or new. But everything applauded immediately is certainly no better than the average intelligence and is therefore something mediocre, dull, regurgitated, or too well digested. As I affirm these Futurist convictions for you, I have the joy of knowing that my talent, my times booed by the audiences of France and Italy, will never be buried beneath too heavy applause. . . Like some Rostand or other![22]

By 1915 the original group of Futurists—Marinetti, Boccioni, Carrà, Balla, Russolo and Severini—had been joined by Ardengo Soffici, painter critic; Giovanni Papini, journalist; Aldo Palazzeschi, poet; Italo Tavolato, writer; Francesca Balilla Pratella, musician; Antonio Saint 'Elia, architect; Enrico Prampolini, painter and stage designer; and Fortunato Depero, painter and stage designer, in addition to a number of minor painters and writers whose overall contribution was negligible. These men were the originators of the creative substance associated with Futurism in their respective fields. Most remained Futurists until after the war although they contributed little between 1916 and 1918, as they were actively involved in the war against Austria and Germany.

Historians are agreed that the vital pre-war years were the most important in terms of Futurist innovation and development both artistically and politically. The political and artistic development of Futurism after 1918 was related to the line of development begun by the Foundation Manifesto of 1909, but was inevitably transformed by Fascism. Certainly in terms of painting and architecture the movement ceases to have much vital material to offer by 1920. Boccioni and Saint 'Elia were killed during the war, and most of the important painters had abandoned the movement as it became more entwined with Mussolini's doctrines. Of the original group of painters, only Balla continued to identify himself with the movement and Marinetti through the 1920's; the other painters who called themselves Futurist were young men who came into the movement after the war who had neither the experiences of the exciting early years nor the talent of their predecessors.

It was only in the areas of music and theatre that Futurism continued to exert a strong influence on other artistic developments. In these fields, the innovations of Marinetti, Russolo, Depero and Prampolini were compelling and important until the end of the "Twenties" when political conditions finally curtailed the opportunity and interest which the post-war boom years had generated. The movement is therefore properly characterized as having two separate phases. The first phase, lasting from 1909 to 1917, included the best and most innovative work accomplished by the Futurists. The second phase, dating from 1918 to 1933, was marked by rampant political outrages on the part of the Futurist-Fasciti and by mediocre art works in the fields of painting, sculpture and architecture. The efforts of Marinetti to keep the movement alive during the second period, and to salvage it from being inextricably bound to Fascism, were manifest in the theatre and in the work done by Luigi Russolo, painter and inventor of "concrete music." The spirit of these works and the impact they had on their respective fields kept alive international interest in the Futurists.

As painting and sculpture in Italy moved away from the axis of Futurist philosophy, Marinetti became more concerned with the evolution of the Futurist Theatre and concentrated his enormous energies on the formulation of complete and comprehensive documents to structure that evolution. Therefore, without examining the second phase of Futurist painting, the balance of this study will be concerned with the impact of Futurist philosophy on the development of the Futurist Theatre aesthetic and with the impact of Futurist painterly principles upon that theatre.

III

PERFORMANCE

Futurism in the theatre has been largely ignored by theatre historians since 1920. John Gassner, for example, in *Theatre In Our Times,* devotes two sentences to the movement, mentioning in each the existence of the movement with others such as Expressionism, Constructivism and Surrealism; each he dismisses as "ventures of variable value and doubtful permanence."[1] The indexes of most standard texts dealing with theatre history do not mention Futurism; Mordecai Gorelik's book on the revolution in modern theatre, for example, does not deal with the movement except to mention it as an antecedent to Surrealism.[2] Therefore, it is reasonable to assume that few students of theatrical art have any comprehension of the unique and important role Futurism has played in the development of modern drama or stage technique. The objectives of this final section of the present study are twofold: to describe Futurist Theatre activities using as a background the political and painterly developments of the preceeding two sections, and to explicate the significant contributions of the Futurist Theatre.

Futurism as a movement consisted of two distinct phases. The first phase, which lasted from 1909 to 1915, was most important and influential in the areas of painting, literature and politics. The second phase, lasting from 1916 to 1929, was characterized by profuse and original theatrical activities while the influence of painting and literature declined. The absorption of Futurism into Fascism which occurred after the war, during 1919, 1920 and 1921, diminished both the potency and the international prestige of the Futurist movement[3] except in the area of theatre art. During this period the Futurist theatre expanded its influence throughout Europe. Two factors caused the eclipse of Futurism under the Fascist regime. The Government exercised control and censorship over the arts, and the artists who had founded and fostered the movement had disavowed Futurism, leaving lesser known, more manipulatable men as standard bearers after 1920.

Activities of a theatrical nature had been customary among the Futurists since 1909, several years prior to the publication of a specific manifesto dealing with Futurist Theatre. The evenings spent declaiming and explicating Futurist political and painting theory, which have been alluded to elsewhere, were in fact planned, staged, and orchestrated by Marinetti. These evenings, called 'serate,'[4] were designed to outrage and provoke that favorite Futurist target "the passatista."[5] Using techniques which the Futurists developed to publicize themselves, their movement and their political ideas, they rented halls or theatres in one city after another, selling tickets to a much touted "opening night." When the audience arrived the Futurists confronted them from the stage with a systematic, thorough and direct attack on their bourgeois mediocrity, passéist ideas and stupidity. The predictable response generally escalated into a melee of shouts, insults, fists, rotten vegetables and finally peaked with the arrival of harried local prefects. Francesco Cangiullo recalls one such 'serate' in Florence at the Verdi Theatre in 1914.

> . . . the showers of potatoes, oranges and bunches of fennel became infernal. Suddenly he [Marinetti] cried, "Damn!" slapping his hand to his eye. We ran to help him; many in the public who had seen the missiles land protested indignantly against bestial cowardice, and, with what we shouted from the stage, the place became a ghetto market where things were said that cannot be repeated, much less written.
>
> I see Russolo again with saliva running from his mouth; I hear Carrà roaring, "Throw an idea instead of potatoes, idiots!" And now the spectators shouted at Filiberto Scarpelli who, to demonstrate solidarity, wished to be with us on stage . . .
>
> I, with a table leg in my hand, wanted to look for a place . . . to support it in the audience.[6]

These evenings, beginning in Turin in 1909, quickly became a Futurist trademark and drew hundreds of curious, angry and sympathetic Italians as the Futurists careened again and again from one end of Italy to the other. As the efficacy of the 'serate' as publicity mechanisms grew, they became more structured, more elaborate and more like performances. Marinetti, aware of the potential for declamation and explication, was also sensitive to an art form buried in the 'serate' which included elements of the cabaret, the theatre and the pulpit.

The first manifesto to deal specifically with Theatre, "The Variety Theatre Manifesto," appeared October 1, 1913 in *Lacerba*. Often called the "Café Concerto" manifesto, it has been republished more often than any other except the "Foundation Manifesto" in 1909 which it greatly resembles in style and spirit. The "Variety Theatre Manifesto," written by Marinetti, was meant to illuminate the direction in which Futurist Theatre activity would proceed. As had been the case with the Futurist painters, comprehension of the task to be accomplished and the possible forms it would take preceeded the actual fact of accomplishment. In this first theatre document Marinetti explicated the task and described the form using the closest available public activities as examples for the principles upon which the new theatre would be based. However, he did not intend the manifesto to be a final statement.[7]

F.T. Marinetti
The Variety Theatre 1913

We are deeply disgusted with the contemporary theatre (verse, prose, and musical) because it vacillates stupidly between historical reconstruction (pastiche or plagiarism) and photographic reproduction of our daily life; a finicking, slow, analytic, and diluted theatre worthy, all in all, of the age of the oil lamp.

FUTURISM EXALTS THE VARIETY THEATRE because:

1. The Variety Theatre, born as we are from electricity, is lucky in having no tradition, no masters, no dogma, and it is fed by swift actuality.

2. The Variety Theatre is absolutely practical, because it proposes to distract and amuse the public with comic effects, erotic stimulation, or imaginative astonishment.

3. The authors, actors, and technicians of the Variety Theatre have only one reason for existing and triumphing: incessantly to invent new elements of astonishment. Hence the absolute impossibility of arresting or repeating oneself, hence an excited competition of brains and muscles to conquer the various records of agility, speed, force, complication, and elegance.

4. The Variety Theatre is unique today in its use of cinema, which enriches it with an incalculable number of visions and otherwise unrealizable spectacles (battles, riots, horse races, automobile and aeroplane meets, trips, voyages, depths of the city, the countryside, oceans, and skies).

5. The Variety Theatre, being a profitable show window for countless inventive forces, naturally generates what I call 'the Futurist marvellous,' produced by modern mechanics. Here are some of the elements of this 'marvellous': (a) powerful caricatures; (b) abysses of the ridiculous; (c) delicious, impalpable ironies; (d) all-embracing, definitive symbols; (e) cascades of uncontrollable hilarity; (f) profound analogies between humanity, the animal, vegetable, and mechanical worlds; (g) flashes of revealing cynicism; (h) plots full of the wit, repartee, and conundrums that aerate the intelligence; (i) the whole gamut of laughter and smiles, to flex the nerves; (j) the whole gamut of stupidity, imbecility, doltishness, and absurdity, insensibly pushing the intelligence to the very border of madness; (k) all the new significations of light, sound, noise, and language, with their mysterious and inexplicable extension into the least-explored part of our sensibility; (l) a cumulus of events unfolded at great speed, of stage characters pushed from right to left in two minutes (and now let's have a look at the Balkans': King Nicolas, Enver-Bey, Daneff, Venizelos, belly-blows and fistfights between Serbs and Bulgars, a *couplet,* and everything vanishes); (m) instructive satirical pantomimes; (n) caricatures of suffering and nostalgia, strongly impressed on the sensibility through gestures exasperating in their spasmodic, hesitant, weary slowness; grave words made ridiculous by funny gestures, bizarre disguises, mutilated words, ugly faces, pratfalls.

6. Today the Variety Theatre is the crucible in which the elements of an emergent new sensibility are seething. Here you find an ironic decomposition of all the worn-out prototypes of the Beautiful, the Grand, the Solemn, the Religious, the Ferocious, the Seductive, and the Terrifying, and also the abstract elaboration of the new prototypes that will succeed these.

The Variety Theatre is thus the synthesis of everything that humanity has up to now refined in its nerves to divert itself by laughing at material and moral grief; it is also the bubbling fusion of all the laughter, all the smiles, all the mocking grins, all the contortions and grimaces of future humanity. Here you sample the joy that will shake men for another century, their poetry, painting, philosophy, and the leaps of their architecture.

7. The Variety Theatre offers the healthiest of all spectacles in its dynamism of form and colour (simultaneous movement of jugglers, ballerinas, gymnasts, colourful riding masters, spiral cyclones of dancers spinning on the points of their feet). In its swift, overpowering dance rhythms the Variety Theatre forcibly drags the slowest souls out of their torpor and forces them to run and jump.

8. The Variety Theatre is alone in seeking the audience's collaboration. It doesn't remain static like a stupid voyeur, but joins noisily in the action, in the singing,

accompanying the orchestra, communicating with the actors in surprising actions and bizarre dialogues. And the actors bicker clownishly with the musicians.

The Variety Theatre uses the smoke of cigars and cigarettes to join the atmosphere of the theatre to that of the stage. And because the audience cooperates in this way with the actors' fantasy, the action develops simultaneously on the stage, in the boxes, and in the orchestra. It continues to the end of the performance, among the battalions of fans, the honeyed dandies who crowd the stage door to fight over the star; double final victory: chic dinner and bed.

9. The Variety Theatre is a school of sincerity for man because it exalts his rapacious instincts and snatches every veil from woman, all the phrases, all the sighs, all the romantic sobs that mask and deform her. On the other hand it brings to light all woman's marvellous animal qualities, her grasp, her powers of seduction, her faithlessness, and her resistance.

10. The Variety Theatre is a school of heroism in the difficulty of setting records and conquering resistances, and it creates on the stage the strong, sane atmosphere of danger. (E.g., death-diving, 'Looping the loop' on bicycles, in cars, and on horseback.)

11. The Variety Theatre is a school of subtlety, complication, and mental synthesis, in its clowns, magicians, mind readers, brilliant calculators, writers of skits, imitators and parodists, its musical jugglers and eccentric Americans, its fantastic pregnancies that give birth to objects and weird mechanisms.

12. The Variety Theatre is the only school that one can recommend to adolescents and to talented young men, because it explains, quickly and incisively, the most abstruse problems and most complicated political events. Example: A year ago at the Folies-Bergere, two dancers were acting out the meandering discussion between Cambon and Kinderlen-Watcher [sic] on the question of Morocco and the Congo in a revealing symbolic dance that was equivalent to at least three years' study of foreign affairs. Facing the audience, their arms entwined, glued together, they kept making mutual territorial concessions, jumping back and forth, to left and right, never separating, neither of them ever losing sight of his goal, which was to become more and more entangled. They gave an impression of extreme courtesy, of skilful, flawlessly diplomatic vacillation, ferocity, diffidence, stubbornness, meticulousness.

Furthermore the Variety Theatre luminously explains the governing laws of life:

(a) the necessity of complication and varying rhythms;

(b) the fatality of the lie and the contradiction (e.g., two-faced English danseuses; little shepherd girl and fearful soldiers);

(c) the omnipotence of a methodical will that modifies human powers;

(d) a synthesis of speed + transformations.

13. The Variety Theatre systematically disparages ideal love and its romantic obsession that repeats the nostalgic languors of passion to satiety, with the robot-like monotony of a daily profession. It whimsically mechanizes sentiment, disparages and healthily tramples down the compulsion towards carnal possession, lowers lust to the natural function of coitus, deprives it of every mystery, every crippling anxiety, every unhealthy idealism.

Instead, the Variety Theater gives a feeling and a taste for easy, light and ironic loves. Café-concert performances in the open air on the terraces of casinos offer a most amusing battle between spasmodic moonlight, tormented by infinite desperations, and the electric light that bounces off the fake jewellery, painted flesh, multicoloured petticoats, velvets, tinsel, the counterfeit colour of his lips. Naturally the energetic electric light triumphs and the soft decadent moonlight is defeated.

14. The Variety Theatre is naturally anti-academic, primitive, and naive, hence the more significant for the unexpectedness of its discoveries and the simplicity of its means. (E.g., the systematic tour of the stage that the *chanteuses* make, like caged animals, at the end of every *couplet.*)

15. The Variety Theatre destroys the Solemn, the Sacred, the Serious, and the Sublime in Art with a capital A. It cooperates in the Futurist destruction of immortal masterworks, plagiarizing them, parodying them, making them look commonplace by stripping them of their solemn apparatus as if they were mere *attractions.* So we unconditionally endorse the performance of *Parsifal* in forty minutes, now in rehearsal in a great London music-hall.

16. The Variety Theatre destroys all our conceptions of perspective, proportion, time, and space. (E.g., a little doorway and gate, thirty centimetres high, alone in the middle of the stage, which certain eccentric Americans open and close as they pass and repass, very seriously as if they couldn't do otherwise.)

17. The Variety Theatre offers us all the records so far attained: the greatest speed and the finest gymnastics and acrobatics of the Japanese, the greatest muscular frenzy of the Negroes, the greatest development of animal intelligence (horses, elephants, seals, dogs, trained birds), the finest melodic inspiration of the Gulf of Naples and the Russian steppes, the best Parisian wit, the greatest competitive force of different races (boxing and wrestling), the greatest anatomical monstrosity, the greatest female beauty.

18. The conventional theatre exalts the inner life, professorial meditation, libraries, museums, monotonous crises of conscience, stupid analyses of feelings, in other words (dirty thing and dirty word), *psychology,* whereas, on the other hand, the Variety Theatre exalts action, heroism, life in the open air, dexterity, the authority of instinct and intuition. To psychology it opposes what I call 'body-madness' *(fisicofollia).*

19. Finally, the Variety Theatre offers to every country (like Italy) that has no great single capital city a brilliant résumé of Paris considered as the one magnetic centre of luxury and ultrarefined pleasure.

FUTURISM WANTS TO TRANSFORM THE VARIETY THEATRE INTO
A THEATRE OF AMAZEMENT, RECORD-SETTING, AND BODY-
MADNESS.

1. One must completely destroy all logic in Variety Theatre performances, exaggerate their luxuriousness in strange ways, multiply contrasts and make the absurd and the unlifelike complete masters of the stage. (Example: Oblige the *chanteuses* to dye their decolletage, orange chignon, etc. Interrupt a song and continue with a revolutionary speech. Spew out a *romanza* of insults and profanity, etc.)

2. Prevent a set of traditions from establishing itself in the Variety Theatre. Therefore oppose and abolish the stupid Parisian 'Revues', as tedious as Greek tragedy with their *Compère* and *Commère* playing the part of the ancient chorus, their parade of political personalities and events set off by wisecracks in a most irritating logical sequence. The Variety Theatre, in fact, must not be what it unfortunately still is today, nearly always a more or less amusing newspaper.

3. Introduce surprise and the need to move among the spectators of the orchestra, boxes, and balcony. Some random suggestions: spread a powerful glue on some of the seats, so that the male or female spectator will stay glued down and make everyone laugh (the damaged frock coat or toilette will naturally be paid for at the door).—

Sell the same ticket to ten people: traffic jam, bickering, and wrangling.—Offer free tickets to gentlemen or ladies who are notoriously unbalanced, irritable, or eccentric and likely to provoke uproars with obscene gestures, pinching women, or other freakishness. Sprinkle the seats with dust to make people itch and sneeze, etc.

4. Systematically prostitute all of classic art on the stage, performing for example all the Greek, French, and Italian tragedies, condensed and comically mixed up, in a single evening.— Put life into the works of Beethoven, Wagner, Bach, Bellini, Chopin, introducing them with Neapolitan songs.—Put Duse, Sarah Bernhardt, Zacconi, Mayol, and Fregoli side by side on the stage.—Play a Beethoven symphony backwards, beginning with the last note.—Boil all of Shakespeare down to a single act. — Do the same with all the most venerated actors. — Have actors recite *Hernani* tied in sacks up to their necks. Soap the floorboards to cause amusing tumbles at the most tragic moments.

5. In every way encourage the *type* of the eccentric American, the impression he gives of exciting grotesquerie, or frightening dynamism; his crude jokes, his enormous brutalities, his trick weskits and pants as deep as a ship's hold out of which, with a thousand other things, will come the great Futurist hilarity that should make the world's face young again.

Because, and don't forget it, we Futurists are YOUNG ARTILLERYMEN ON A TOOT, as we proclaimed in our manifesto, 'Let's Murder the Moonshine', fire + fire + light against moonshine and against old firmaments war every night great cities to blaze with electric signs. Immense black face (30 metres high + 150 metres height of the building = 180 metres) open close open close a golden eye 3 metres high SMOKE SMOKE MANOLI SMOKE MANOLI CIGARETTES woman in a blouse (50 metres + 120 metres of building = 170 metres) stretch relax a violet rosy lilac blue bust broth of electric light in a champagne glass (30 metres) sizzle evaporate in a mouthful of darkness electric signs dim die under a dark stiff hand come to life again continue stretch out in the night the human day's activity courage + folly never to die or cease or sleep electric signs = formation and disaggregation of mineral and vegetable centre of the earth circulation of blood in the ferrous faces of Futurist houses increases, empurples (joy anger more more still stronger) as soon as the negative pessimist sentimental nostalgic shadows besiege the city brilliant revival of streets that channel a smoky swarm of workers by day two horses (30 metres tall) rolling golden balls with their hoofs GIOCONDA PURGATIVE WATERS crisscross of *trrr trrrr* Elevated *trrr trrrr* overhead trrrombone whissstle ambulance sirens and firetrucks transformation of the streets into splendid corridors to guide, push logic necessity the crowd towards trepidation + laughter + music-hall uproar FOLIES-BERGERE EMPIRE CREME-ECLIPSE tubes of mercury red red red blue violet huge letter-eels of gold purple diamond fire Futurist defiance to the weepy night the stars' defeat warmth enthusiasm faith conviction will power penetration of an electric sign into the house across the street *yellow slaps* for that gouty, dozy bibliophile in slippers 3 mirrors watch him the sign plunges to 3 redgold abysses open close open close 3 thousand metres deep horror quick go out out hat stick steps taximeter push shove *zuu zuoeu* here we are dazzle of the promenade solemnity of the panther-cocottes in their comic-opera tropics fat warm smell of music-hall gaiety = tireless ventilation of the world's Futurist brain.[8]

In describing the Variety Theatre, Marinetti used the music-hall, cabaret, night club, athletic event and circus as models upon which the new theatre would be based. He did not call the Variety Theatre a Futurist Theatre, but rather the starting point for the formation of a Futurist Theatre which would contain many of the attributes synthesized from public entertainment as he saw it in 1913. In so far as many of these entertainment forms were thoroughly modern, complex and technical, they contained elements which Marinetti believed were useful and appropriate to Futurism. Marinetti intended these ersatz performance methods to provide a stimulus for the development of Futurist Theatre which would be synthesized from many sources. He called the Variety Theatre "the crucible in which the elements of a new sensibility that is coming into being are stirring."[9] In this first theatre manifesto of 1913, Marinetti suggested a developmental growth of a Futurist Theatre which would be constantly regenerated and renovated, a theatre which would not remain fixed stylistically but which would evolve beyond any prescribed system, style or 'raison d'être'.

The basic philosophy underlying the "Variety Theatre Manifesto" and the Futurist Theatre forms which derived from it between the years 1913 and 1925 were inherent in the Foundation Manifesto of 1909. For example, Marinetti was particularly delighted with the physical, energetic, competitive aspects of the Variety Theatre; the robust humor of vaudeville, the speed and danger of death-diving, the grace and agility of gymnasts. In these he found reflections of the "aggressive movement, feverish insomnia, the running step, the somersault, the insult and pinches"[10] of his Foundation Manifesto.

The spectacles provided by the Variety Theatre existed in and of themselves, irrespective of what preceeded or followed each segment of a performance. There was no necessary order of appearance, no thread or narrative carrying the spectator from one act to the next. This structure of unrelated activities strung together for the entertainment of the audience was fundamental to what Marinetti viewed as the true form which Futurist Theatre would eventually achieve.

In calling for an end to well made plays, contrivances, psychologies, denouements, and all the other accoutrements of the established theatre, he proposed what has been termed 'illogical theatre'. Illogical theatre allowed events and incidents to occur without regard to their relationship to one another, or to their consequences. In effect, Marinetti initiated a theatre which eliminated cause and effect, where audience expectancy and rules of probability exerted no influence on stage actions. The concept of illogical structure which was articulated in the Variety Theatre Manifesto had been developed in Marinetti's poetry, from which it pervaded all forms of Futurist literature. Marinetti believed that the audience was not to be permitted to proceed in its accustomed manner of putting together information in a logical sequence. The new Futurist Theatre, which would come into being, would teach the audience to intuit information, sensation and understanding. The Variety Theatre's illogical structure was an elementary step towards the instruction of the intuitive approach to the audience.

The intuitive approach to art was one of the most important of Marinetti's dictums. It was fundamental to his literary, theatrical and cinematic manifestos, as well as to the manifestos of the painters and sculptors, although it was not always included formally in these works. For Marinetti and the Futurists, a paramount task was the stimulation of the passéist intuitive capability.

> Intuition [was] the quality which enabled one to discover analogies which although hidden to reason, yet are the essentials of art. Analogy is but another name for that immense love which brings distant things into close relationship. Poets have always been aware of the possibilities of analogy. Their difficulty was that they kept too close to external resemblances and did not venture to take those daring leaps made possible by intuition.[11]

Andrego Soffici, art critic and historian, wrote a rebuttal of an attack on Futurism made by the famous philosopher Benedetto Croce. In his rebuttal Soffici explained the inseparable and mystic nature of the creative process, which he called a combination of unconscious inspiration (intuition), and intellectual discipline, which he called lucid volition.

> Poetry and the other arts display values which cannot be accounted for in abstract logical terms. There is no appraising system of esthetics outside the terms of art itself; every attempt to construct one has resulted in the evaluation not of artistic qualities but of extraneous matters. Poetry does not proceed from knowledge and knowledge can in no way be made its aim, unless by knowledge we mean the inspired intuitional enjoyment of the reader which is but a resonance of the original super-rational creative act of the poet.[12]

These principles which the Futurists expounded for the writing of Futurist poetry were also transferred to Futurist dramatic literature as well as to film scripts. In various ways these principles modified both the written playscript and its performance.

Just as the painters had found it necessary to develop new methods of utilizing the available means of expression, so did the writers. The 'parole in libertà' was one such innovation which in a broad sense affected all traditional forms of literary structure by freeing the writer from all regulation. The 'parole in libertà' (words in freedom) was a basic unit of illogical literature, an extension of free verse which eliminated the rules of versification, syntax, spelling and typography. The 'parole in libertà' is perhaps best described by developing a parallel between the function of 'parole in libertà' in literature and the force-lines in Futurist painting, discussed in the preceding section of this study.

'Parole in libertà' were used to suggest the object and its ramifications in terms of writing. For example, the modifiers grey, stormy, disgusting, placed together in parentheses at the beginning of a clause, create a swiftly comprehended coloration for the substantives that follow: passengers, sea, ship, sky, decks, nausea. Force-lines, as described previously, are the "representation of the movements of matter along the trajectory determined by the structure of the object and its action. This direction enfolds the colored volumes which create chromatic form in its infinite mobility."[13] In other words, the force-lines are used as modifiers of the objects used in the composition. The process expected of the reader in compiling the messages from the 'parole in libertà' and the process used to compile the messages stimulated by the force-lines are similar. In both cases the spectator is required to repress his usual cerebral linear reading function and submit to an unordered bombarding of his perceptual faculties. By repressing his normal perceptual process, the spectator or reader intuits and absorbs the messages coming from the Futurist canvas or printed page.

The abolition of syntax was inherent in the use of 'parole in libertà'. It was embraced by the Futurists who used it to lead them to further assaults on the written form. The end of syntax, so they contended, implied the end of conjugations. Conjugations were replaced by the superior infinitive; "The infinitive is round, and like a wheel it may be applied to all other cars of the analogical train; by making stops impossible it provides style with speed. Moods and tenses are rectangular, square, or oval. The infinitive alone is circular."[14]

In further efforts to increase the speed with which the reader could be impinged upon by the writer's words, the Futurists abolished punctuation partly replacing it by mathematical signs such as $\times$ $+$ $:$ $-$ $=$ $>$ $<$, or by another device which had a certain popularity, the use of musical indications such as piu presto, rallentando, and due tempi. These two devices were used in two ways: either as marginal notes to assist the reader to gain the proper sense of speed or rhythm, or as inclusions in the text to impart the same information in a more imperative manner. Moreover, musical indications were most frequently employed where their inherent musical connotation would be of use to the poet in invoking melody or rhythm.[15] Mathematical signs seem to appear where they provide an element of surprise or interruption.

On another level both the musical indications and the use of mathematical signs was perhaps aimed at bringing into play "the simultaneousness of states of mind in the work of art," which had been the professed aim of the painters. It would be unlikely that the reader could suppress the interaction of mathematical or musical notions with the word sensations on the page. In this way an overlapping of stimuli was accomplished; words, which evoked their own series of images upon the brain, coincided with sensations from the more subtle art of music. A third stimulus was provided by the suggestion of mathematical relationships.

Another literary means of evoking the intuitive response which, like the use of musical indications, was very much involved with sound, was a distortion of words as part of "integral onomatopoeia." Through word distortion the Futurists developed an onomatopoetic system which included the formation of sounds which had no specific similarity to significant words. The system could be direct or imitative. For example, the direct use of onomatopoeia was the use of word-sounds such as 'boom' or 'miau'. The imitative use of onomatopoeia was described by Marinetti:

> In my *Zang-Tumb-Tumb* the strident onomatopoeia ssii, which reproduces the whistle of a tugboat on the Meuse, is followed by the muffled fiiufiiu coming from the other bank. These two onomatopoeias have enabled me to dispense with the description of the breadth of the river which is measured by contrasting the consonants s and f.[16]

Prefiguring the Surrealists by several years, the Futurists devised two more systems of word-sounds which they called indirect onomatopoeia and abstract onomatopoeia. The former was used to express one's subjective responses to external conditions, the latter "served to echo the complex and obscure movement of the soul without reference to external sound or movements." Both systems were inappropriate to dramatic literature. They do, however, reflect the idea of interior motion which concerned the painters.

One of Marinetti's literary innovations had a primarily visual impact, the 'typographic revolution'. Marinetti was especially proud of the 'typographic revolution' about which he said:

> This new array of type, this variety of colors, this original use of characters enable me to increase many times the expressive power of words. By this practice I combat the decorative and 'precious' style of Mallarmé, his recherché language.[17] I also combat Mallarmé's static ideal. My reformed typesetting allows me to treat words like torpedoes and to hurl them forth at all speeds: at the velocity of stars, clouds, aeroplanes, trains, waves, explosives, molecules, atoms.[18]

The typography which the Futurists devised combined letters in Italic, Roman, Gothic; of small, medium and large size; and utilized different color schemes, all in varying formations. Soffici maintained that the letters themselves were beautiful even after they had been submerged in the alphabetic series.

> The letters have an extraordinary power of suggestion; they evoke past civilizations, dead languages. Their beauty may be enhanced by pictorial practices which, however, do not go beyond the means and instruments of the typesetter. Changes in size, arrangement, and color give the requisite movement to a page which then may, with justification, be called a work of art.[19]

The importance of the typographic revolution and its usefulness were celebrated in a short play by Balla called *Printing Press* (Macchina Tipografica) written and staged in 1914. The set, pictured in Figure 1, demonstrated the possibilities of typeset. Balla painted his giant letters onto the wings and back-drop in a mock-perspective manner. Against the backdrop, the performers, various parts of the typesetting machine, performed a series of mechanized movements in imitation of the machine in operation. The mechanized machine idea was to influence a large number of theatre practitioners over the next twenty years. Balla's simple, naive rendering (Figure 2) may have been the first example of "machine theatre." The Futurists were most energetic in their pursuit of the 'mechanized theatre'.

Onomatopoeia, typography, 'parole in libertà' and abolition of syntax were combined with several performance techniques which evolved from the 'serate,' with techniques for declaiming poetry and propaganda, and with elements of the Variety Theatre. All innovations worked out in one discipline were available to the Futurists of all of the other disciplines and there was an astounding amount of transfer and translation of information between artists. This practice of integrating principles from one art form with another and translating the fundamental ideas of the movement into usable artistic vocabularies gave Futurism a stylistic homogeneity.

The most obvious consequence of Futurist literary devices which were transposed into the writing of plays was the incoherence of the play when compared to traditional, explicit, dramatic literature. (Usually plays written in the new Futurist style were performed by the Futurists, or by closely tutored friends, who could comprehend the material and convey it properly.) However, the central purpose of these innovations in literature which had been adapted to playscripts was to begin the process of abstracting out of the play all the essential features. Characters lost their personalities and became abbreviated in a manner which imbued them with a mechanical aspect. This mechanical character concept, perhaps derived from Gordon Craig,[20] developed into a major concern among the Futurists. Plot became shortened and intensified so that a single incident might be all the action utilized.

An early play of Marinetti's, dated 1913, describes a young woman who enters an office, sits down and converses with a man of no description.[21] The dialogue contains no information about either character, gives no reason for their activity and has only a faint resemblance to anything which might actually take place. On a sound from off stage, the young woman rises and leaves and the play ends. There are other signals which are indicated by marginal notes and which have ambiguous meanings. The dialogue has the same sparseness of the 'parole in libertà'. Also at certain points the reader gets the feeling that they are about to begin talking with each other in a logical sequential way, but it never quite occurs. Very rich images are passed between them, but the images have no function. The mechanical nature of the actors is reinforced by the single author's note at the bottom of the script which requests that the actors move with deliberation and in no way express any emotion in what they are doing or saying.

These short early plays written between 1910 and 1914 had the illogical and non-sequential aspect called for in Marinetti's "Variety Theatre Manifesto," and contained little psychological or character development. Some seemed to depict social types such as the wealthy art patron, the socialite, the debonair bachelor, and the fat politician. Plot was minimal, involving one or two incidents and no climactic event. Indeed, these plays had no clear message, no theme, no exposition, no denouement. The most that can be said of them is that they occasionally had humor and that they were capable of rendering a very small vignette of some everyday aspect of life.

Prior to 1914, the performances given by the Futurists lacked a clearly recognizable form. Several types of structure were used for different purposes. The 'serate,' which constituted the major form of production, could consist of poetry readings, political discourses, lectures, art shows, riots or even plays. These performances, or 'serate,' were distinguished by their lack of form and by the inclusion of multiple performance techniques such as juggling, dancing, and contests of various sorts. This loose and unpredictable structure was in keeping with the style of performance which Marinetti found admirable in the "Variety Theatre Manifesto."

Before 1914 there was no coherent production design guiding Futurist performances; many aspects of these performances were spontaneously arranged at the last moment. For example, arriving in Turin for an evening of lectures in 1913, Marinetti found that the rented hall had no curtain separating stage from auditorium. He had planned on having several Futurists, hidden from the audience, call out certain responses to questions in his lecture and later to appear and take part in the discussion which would follow. In order to provide himself with a means of carrying out his plan, he dashed out during the afternoon and bought ten folding Japanese screens which he lined up on stage behind his lectern. The effect was apparently hilarious as the audience had a view of the legs and shoes of the waiting Futurists. This same effect was later developed into a short theatre piece called *Feet* in which various lower legs performed improvisations together while the rest of the bodies were concealed behind a semi-lowered curtain.

The Futurists had discovered an effective and useful method of decorating the stage space during the early years of the movement. Wishing to display their work and surround themselves with a "Futurist milieu,"[22] they hung Futurist paintings along the drops to form a "painted backdrop" against which the action occurred, as in Figure 4. This custom continued through the history of the movement and has been cited by a number of journalists and scholars. The hanging paintings were often well received by critics and audiences and they were frequently sold after the performannce. The custom of hanging paintings does not constitute a design scheme; the possibilities for stage design were not developed in these early performances. The only mention of concern for the stage space appears in the "Variety Theatre Manifesto":

> 16. The Variety Theatre destroys all our conceptions of perspective, proportion, time and space. (E.g., a little doorway and gate, thirty centimetres high, alone in the middle of the stage, which certain eccentric Americans open and close as they pass and repass, very seriously as if they couldn't do otherwise.)[23]

During 1914 Marinetti developed some of the areas of performance which had been neglected in the 'serate' and which are not expressly described in the "Variety Theatre Manifesto." Marinetti, assisted by the Futurist painters, demonstrated a scenographic compliment to performance, a mode of dressing the stage which would be integral to whatever activity they planned. They were not consistent in their use of scenography, nor were they always original in their selection of scenographic elements. They were exploring the possibilities of the space and especially the relationship between the performance space and the audience which had been of central importance in Marinetti's "Variety Theatre Manifesto."

An early example of the use of scenographic elements in a performance occurred in Rome in March and April of 1914. The Futurists performed what they termed an evening of "dynamic and synoptic declamation," or an evening of poetry readings sometimes accompanied by multiple voices and instrumental sounds. For this performance Marinetti read from the 'parole in libertà' poem *Piedigrotta* by Francesco Cangiullo. The performance was held at the Spovieri Gallery in Rome. The gallery was actually a large hall hung with numerous Futurist canvases and a large drop curtain painted by Balla, Boccioni, Severini, Carrà and Russolo. A large freestanding set-piece which depicted three "Crocean philosophers"[24] adorned one corner of the hall. The room was lit with lights covered with red paper which created an effect variously called "adulterated chianti,"[25] "bloody and dim"[26] and "murky."[27] The light quality was given special attention by Marinetti who wished to use the light to "erase the old distinctions between areas, compartments of people."[28] Consequently, the hall was treated as one space which contained both performers and patrons. The performers were the Futurists themselves attired in splendid costumes capped with rich and exotic hats. The declamation was carried out by Marinetti with various amounts of choral support from Balla and Cangiullo. Moreover, the recitation was enhanced by orchestration from several homemade instruments which were used to generate a panoply of sounds many of which were unmusical.[29] Clearly, the Futurist performances of 1914 had moved away from the Variety Theatre's casual production style in that these evenings had a cohesiveness and planned program which integrated the efforts of the

Figure 1

Design by Balla for his *Printing Press* (*Macchina Tipografica*, 1914).
(From a reproduction in *Futurist Performance* by Michael Kirby
[New York: E.P. Dutton and Co., Inc., 1971].)

Figure 2

Perhaps the earliest examples of "mechanized performers."
Sketches by Balla for *Printing Press* (*Macchina Tipografica,* 1914).
(From a reproduction in *Futurist Performance* by Michael Kirby
[New York: E.P. Dutton and Co., Inc., 1971].)

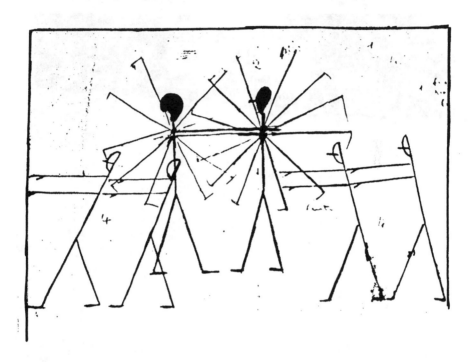

Figure 3

Photograph from the production *Feet* by Marinetti, 1915.
(From a reproduction in *Futurist Performance* by Michael Kirby
[New York: E.P. Dutton and Co., Inc., 1972] .)

Figure 4

Pictures and words-in-freedom by Depero. Rome, 1916.
(From *Futurist Manifestos* by Umbro Apollonio
[New York: Viking Press, 1973].)

poets and painters toward a production design. Moreover, performance space, ignored in the "Variety Theatre Manifesto," had become an integral aspect of the Futurist performance, requiring some consideration and design. The introduction of Futurist 'noise' and a Futurist chorus into the performances aroused possibilities which were developed later as the full force of Futurist Theatre began to emerge.

  Early in 1915, Marinetti, with Bruno Corra and Emilio Settimelli, wrote the "Futurist Synthetic Theatre Manifesto," published in Milan on January 11. The "Futurist Synthetic Theatre Manifesto" announced and explicated the core of ideas from which theatre activity subsequently derived. Unlike the "Variety Theatre Manifesto" which had proposed tentative resources and possible directions to be explored in an effort to evolve a Futurist Theatre aesthetic, the Futurist Synthetic Theatre Manifesto was the definitive statement which had been promised two years earlier.

F.T. Marinetti, Emilio Settimelli, Bruno Corra
THE FUTURIST SYNTHETIC THEATRE 1915

As we await our much prayed-for great war, we Futurists carry our violent anti-neutralist action from city square to university and back again, using our art to prepare the Italian sensibility for the great hour of maximum danger. Italy must be fearless, eager, as swift and elastic as a fencer, as indifferent to blows as a boxer, as impassive at the news of a victory that may have cost fifty thousand dead as at the news of a defeat.

  For Italy to learn to make up its mind with lightening speed, to hurl itself into battle, to sustain every undertaking and every possible calamity, books and reviews are unnecessary. They interest and concern only a minority, are more or less tedious, obstructive, and relaxing. They cannot help chilling enthusiasm, aborting impulses, and poisoning with doubt a people at war. War—Futurism intensified—obliges us to march and not to rot [*marciare, non marcire*] in libraries and reading rooms. THERFORE WE THINK THAT THE ONLY WAY TO INSPIRE ITALY WITH THE WARLIKE SPIRIT TODAY IS THROUGH THE THEATRE. In fact ninety percent of Italians go to the theatre, whereas only ten percent read books and reviews. But what is needed is a FUTURIST THEATRE, completely opposed to the passeist theatre that drags its monotonous, depressing processions around the sleepy Italian stages.

  Not to dwell on this historical theatre, a sickening genre already abandoned by the passeist public, we condemn the whole contemporary theatre because it is too prolix, analytic, pedantically psychological, explanatory, diluted, finicking, static, as full of prohibitions as a police station, as cut up into cells as a monastery, as moss-grown as an old abandoned house. In other words it is a pacifistic, neutralist theatre, the antithesis of the fierce, overwhelming, synthesizing velocity of the war.

Our Futurist Theatre will be:

Synthetic. That is, very brief. To compress into a few minutes, into a few words and gestures, innumerable situations, sensibilities, ideas, sensations, facts, and symbols.

The writers who wanted to renew the theatre (Ibsen, Maeterlinck, Andreyev, Claudel, Shaw) never thought of arriving at a true synthesis, of freeing themselves from a technique that involves prolixity, meticulous analysis, drawn-out preparation. Before the works of these authors, the audience is in the indignant attitude of a circle of bystanders who swallow their anguish and pity as they watch the slow agony of a horse who has collapsed on the pavement. The sigh of applause that finally breaks out frees the audience's stomach from all the indigestible time it has swallowed. Each act is as painful as having to wait patiently in an antechamber for the minister (*coup de théâtre:* kiss, pistol shot, verbal revelation, etc.) to receive you. All this passéist or semi-Futurist theatre, instead of synthesizing fact and idea in the smallest number of words and gestures, savagely destroys the variety of place (source of dynamism and amazement), stuffs many city squares, landscapes, streets, into the sausage of a single room. For this reason this theatre is entirely static.

We are convinced that mechanically, by force of brevity, we can achieve an entirely new theatre perfectly in tune with our swift and laconic Futurist sensibility. Our acts can also be moments [*attiattimi*] only a few seconds long. With this essential and synthetic brevity the theatre can bear and even overcome competition from the cinema.

Atechnical. The passéist theatre is the literary form that most distorts and diminishes an author's talent. This form, much more than lyric poetry or the novel, is subject to *the demands of technique:* (1) to omit every notion that doesn't conform to public taste; (2) once a theatrical idea has been found (expressible in a few pages), to stretch it out over two, three or four acts; (3) to surround an interesting character with many pointless types: coat-holders, door-openers, all sorts of bizarre comic turns; (4) to make the length of each act vary between half and three-quarters of an hour; (5) to construct each act taking care to (a) begin with seven or eight absolutely useless pages, (b) introduce a tenth of your idea in the first act, five-tenths in the second, four tenths in the third, (c) shape your acts for rising excitement, each act being no more than a preparation for the finale, (d) always make the first act a *little boring* so that the second act can be *amusing* and the third *devouring;* (6) to set off every *essential* line with a hundred or more insignificant *preparatory* lines; (7) never to devote less than a page to explaining an entrance or an exit minutely; (8) to apply systematically to the whole play *the role of a superficial variety,* to the acts, scenes, and lines. For instance, to make one act a day, another an evening, another deep night; to make one act pathetic, another anguished, another sublime; when you have to prolong a dialogue between two actors, make something happen to interrupt it, a falling vase, a passing mandolin player. . . . Or else have the actors constantly move around from sitting to standing, from right to left, and meanwhile vary the dialogue to make it seem as if a bomb might explode outside at any moment (e.g., the betrayed husband might catch his wife red-handed) when actually nothing is going to explode until the end of the act; (9) to be enormously careful about *the verisimilitude of the plot;* (10) to write your play in such a manner that *the audience understands in the finest detail the how and why of everything that takes place on the stage, above all that it knows by the last act how the protagonists will end up.*

With our synthetist movement in the theatre, we want to destroy the Technique that from the Greeks until now, instead of simplifying itself, has become more and more dogmatic, stupid, logical, meticulous, pedantic, struggling. THEREFORE:

1. *It's stupid to write one hundred pages where one would do,* only because the audience through habit and infantile instinct wants to see character in a play result from a series of events, wants to fool itself into thinking that the character really exists in order to admire the beauties of Art, meanwhile refusing to acknowledge any art if the author limits himself to sketching out a few of the character's traits.

2. *It's stupid* not to rebel against the prejudice of theatricality when life itself (which consists *of actions vastly more awkward, uniform, and predictable* than those that unfold in the world of art) is for the most part *antitheatrical* and even in this offers *innumerable possibilities for the stage.* EVERYTHING OF ANY VALUE IS THEATRICAL.

3. *It's stupid* to pander to the primitivism of the crowd, which, in the last analysis, wants to see the bad guy lose and the good guy win.

4. *It's stupid* to worry about verisimilitude (absurd because talent and worth have little to do with it).

5. *It's stupid* to want to explain with logical minuteness everything taking place on the stage, when even in life one never grasps an event entirely, in all its causes and consequences, because reality throbs around us, bombards us *with squalls of fragments of inter-connected events, mortised and tenoned together, confused, mixed up, chaotic.* E.g. it's stupid to act out a contest between two persons *always* in an orderly, clear, and logical way, since in daily life we nearly always encounter mere *flashes of argument* made *momentary* by our modern experience, in a tram, a cafe, a railway station, which remain cinematic in our minds like fragmentary dynamic symphonies of gestures, words, lights, and sounds.

6. *It's stupid* to submit to obligatory *crescendi, prepared effects,* and *postponed climaxes.*

7. *It's stupid* to allow one's talent to be burdened with the weight of a technique that *anyone* (even imbeciles) *can acquire by study, practice, and patience.*

8. IT'S STUPID TO RENOUNCE THE DYNAMIC LEAP IN THE VOID OF TOTAL CREATION, BEYOND THE RANGE OF TERRITORY PREVIOUSLY EXPLORED.

Dynamic, simultaneous. That is, born of improvisation, lightning-like intuition, from suggestive and revealing actuality. We believe that a thing is valuable to the extent that it is improvised (hours, minutes, seconds), not extensively prepared (months, years, centuries).

We feel an unconquerable repugnance for desk work, *a priori,* that fails to respect the ambience of the theatre itself. THE GREATER NUMBER OF OUR WORKS HAVE BEEN WRITTEN IN THE THEATRE. The theatrical ambience is our inexhaustible reservoir of inspirations: the magnetic circular sensation invading our tired brains during morning rehearsal in an empty gilded theatre; an actor's intonation that suggests the possibility of constructing a cluster of paradoxical thoughts on top of it; a movement of scenery that hints at a symphony of lights; an actress's fleshiness that fills our minds with genially full-bodied notions.

We overran Italy at the head of a heroic battalion of comedians who imposed on audiences *Elettricità* and other Futurist syntheses (alive yesterday, today surpassed and condemned by us) that were revolutions imprisoned in auditoriums.—From the Politeama Garibaldi of Palermo to the Dal Verme of Milan. The Italian theatres smoothed the wrinkles in the raging massage of the crowd and rocked with bursts of volcanic laughter. We fraternized with the actors. Then, on sleepless nights in trains, we argued, goading each other to heights of genius to the rhythm of tunnels and stations. Our Futurist theatre jeers at Shakespeare but pays attention to the gossip of actors, is put to sleep by a line from Ibsen but is inspired by red or green reflections from the stalls. WE ACHIEVE AN ABSOLUTE DYNAMISM THROUGH THE INTERPENETRATION OF DIFFERENT ATMOSPHERES AND TIMES. E.g., whereas in a drama like *Più che L'Amore* [D'Annunzio], the important events (for instance, the murder of the gambling-house keeper) don't take place on the stage but are narrated with a complete lack of dynamism; and in the first act of *La Figlia di Jorio* [D'Annunzio] the events take place against a simple background with no jumps in space or time; in the Futurist synthesis, *Simultaneita,* there are two ambiences that interpenetrate and many different times put into action simultaneously.

Autonomous, alogical, unreal. The Futurist theatrical synthesis will not be subject to logic, will pay no attention to photography; it will be *autonomous,* will resemble nothing but itself, although it will take elements from reality and combine them as its whim dictates. Above all, just as the painter and composer discover, scattered through the outside world, a narrower but more intense life, made up of colours, forms, sounds, and noises, the same is true *for the man gifted with theatrical sensibility, for whom a specialized reality exists that violently assaults his nerves:* it consists of what is called THE THEATRICAL WORLD.

THE FUTURIST THEATRE IS BORN OF THE TWO MOST VITAL CURRENTS in the Futurist sensibility, defined in the two manifestos 'The Variety Theatre' and 'Weights, Measures, and Prices of Artistic Genius,' which are: (1) our frenzied passion for real, swift, elegant, complicated, cynical muscular, fugitive, Futurist life; (2) our very modern cerebral definition of art according to which no logic, no tradition, no aesthetic, no technique, no opportunity can be imposed on the artist's natural talent; he must be preoccupied only with creating synthetic expressions of cerebral energy that have THE ABSOLUTE VALUE OF NOVELTY.

The *Futurist theatre* will be able to excite its audience, that is make it forget the monotony of daily life, by sweeping it through a *labyrinth of sensations imprinted on the most exacerbated originality and combined in unpredictable ways.*

Every night the *Futurist theatre* will be a gymnasium to train our race's spirit to the swift, dangerous enthusiasms made necessary by this Futurist year.

CONCLUSIONS

1. TOTALLY ABOLISH THE TECHNIQUE THAT IS KILLING THE PASSÉIST THEATRE.

2. DRAMATIZE ALL THE DISCOVERIES (no matter how unlikely, weird, and antitheatrical) THAT OUR TALENT IS DISCOVERING IN THE SUBCONSCIOUS, IN ILL-DEFINED FORCES, IN PURE ABSTRACTION, IN THE PURELY CEREBRAL, THE PURELY FANTASTIC, IN RECORD-SETTING AND BODYMADNESS. (E.g., *Vengono,* F.T. Marinetti's first drama of objects, a new vein of theatrical sensibility discovered by Futurism.)

3. SYMPHONIZE THE AUDIENCE'S SENSIBILITY BY EXPLORING IT, STIRRING UP ITS LAZIEST LAYERS WITH EVERY MEANS POSSIBLE; ELIMINATE THE PRECONCEPTION OF THE FOOTLIGHTS BY THROWING NETS OF SENSATION BETWEEN STAGE AND AUDIENCE; THE STAGE ACTION WILL INVADE THE ORCHESTRA, SETS, THE AUDIENCE.

4. FRATERNIZE WARMLY WITH THE ACTORS WHO ARE AMONG THE FEW THINKERS WHO FLEE FROM EVERY DEFORMING CULTURAL ENTERPRISE.

5. ABOLISH THE FARCE, THE VAUDEVILLE, THE SKETCH, THE COMEDY, THE SERIOUS DRAMA, AND TRAGEDY, AND CREATE IN THEIR PLACE THE MANY FORMS OF FUTURIST THEATRE, SUCH AS: LINES WRITTEN IN FREE WORDS, SIMULTANEITY, INTERPENETRATION, THE SHORT, ACTED-OUT POEM, THE DRAMATIZED SENSATION, COMIC DIALOGUE, THE NEGATIVE ACT, THE REECHOING LINE, 'EXTRA-LOGICAL' DISCUSSION, SYNTHETIC DEFORMATION, THE SCIENTIFIC OUTBURST THAT CLEARS THE AIR.
6. THROUGH UNBROKEN CONTACT, CREATE BETWEEN US AND THE CROWD A CURRENT OF CONFIDENCE RATHER THAN RESPECTFULNESS, IN ORDER TO INSTILL IN OUR AUDIENCES THE DYNAMIC VIVACITY OF A NEW FUTURIST THEATRICALITY.

These are the *first* words on the theatre. Our first eleven theatrical syntheses (by Marinetti, Settimelli, Bruno Corra, R. Chiti, Balilla Pratella) were victoriously imposed on crowded theatres in Ancona, Bologna, Padua, Naples, Venice, Verona, Florence, and Roma, by Ettore Berti, Zoncada, and Petrolini. In Milan we soon shall have the great metal building, enlivened by all the electro-mechanical inventions, that alone will permit us to realize our freest conceptions on the stage.[30]

The "Futurist Synthetic Theatre Manifesto" was by proclamation the first word on the Futurist theatre. Combining elements from the "Variety Theatre Manifesto," from the 'serate,' from other manifestos (e.g., "Weights and Measures," "Photodynamism," "Manifesto to Playwrights") and from their experiences over the last two years, Marinetti, Corra and Settimelli defined the Futurist theatre aesthetic which had been promised in the "Variety Theatre Manifesto" which said, "Today the Variety Theatre is the crucible in which the elements of an emergent new sensibility are seething."

An important aspect of the "Futurist Synthetic Theatre Manifesto" was the political emphasis incorporated into it. Marinetti believed emphatically in the propaganda potential of theatre, potential which he and the Futurists were committed to exploiting in their efforts to engage Italy in the War. The Pact of London, officially allying Italy with England and France against the Triple Alliance Nations, an objective which was paramount to Marinetti and the Futurists, was signed just five months after the manifesto was written. Unmistakably the Manifesto was part of an all-out campaign launched by the Futurists between January 1915 and August 1916 to proselytize and promote the war through a barrage of activities, principally theatre. Futurist performers toured the length and breadth of the Italian peninsula, playing to generally receptive and boisterous audiences. During the months of February, March, April and May eight companies were recorded touring a repertory of Futurist productions.

Although the Futurists were pledged to preparing Italy for war, the activities which followed the publication of the manifesto were not confined to war themes or to propagandist content. The physical and intellectual revolution which the Futurists proposed was expedited by the imminence of the war but not dependent on it. Rather, Futurism at this vital, energetic stage of growth was greater in scope and ambition than is usually acknowledged by historians. The Futurists saw themselves as prophets struggling against a massive wave of inert humanity which must be jabbed and pummeled onward into the future and which must be able to advance unencumbered by vestigial pre-Futurist drawbacks such as religion, fear, education, conditioning and bourgeois value systems. In fact, the Futurists, with the jabbing and pummelling created an atmosphere of "feverish creativity," "jarred awareness," "speed, noise and bodymadness" which involved all levels of society encouraging their participation and gaining their committment. The radical political motivation behind Marinetti's movement, with its attendant passion and zeal, ran contrary to the detached and effete intellectualism that had been characteristic of art groups before the emergence of Futurism. The Futurists were the vanguard of a new wave of art movements whose political philosophies would include the conversion of the masses through the arts, notably Dada and Surrealism.

For the Futurists, theatre was considered the most efficiacious means for transmitting to the inert masses the new ideology: "Every night the Futurist Theatre will be a gymnasium to train our race's spirit to the swift, dangerous enthusiasms made necessary by this Futurist year. . . The Futurist Theatre will be able to excite its audience, that is, make it forget the monotony of daily life, by sweeping it through a labyrinth of sensations imprinted on the most exacerbated originality and combined in unpredictable ways."[31] The Futurist Synthetic Theatre Manifesto described the techniques for accomplishing this objective.

The basic unit of the Futurist Synthetic Theatre was a short compressed script called a 'sintesi'. The essential feature of the 'sintesi' was its briefness, a few lines to a few pages at most.

> The Futurist Theatre was to express in a very few minutes and with a very few words and gestures innumerable situations, emotions, ideas, sensations and facts, and to present a tragedy in sixty acts of which the first fifty-nine need not be shown.[32]

An example of the compression of time, character development and dialogue typical of the 'sintesi' occurs in *Education* by Angelo Rognoni.

A classroom.

THE PROFESSOR (thirty years old. He is reading to his students.): Dante is a great poet. He wrote the "Divine Comedy" and . . .

(Several seconds of darkness.)

THE PROFESSOR (forty years old. He is reading with a bored voice): Dante is a great poet. He wrote the "Divine Comedy" and . . .

(Several seconds of silence.)

THE PROFESSOR (sixty years old. He is like a gramophone.): Dante is a great poet. . .

A PUPIL (interrupting him): Why?

THE PROFESSOR (surprised and embarrassed): It is printed here. Sit down and be quiet. Dante is a great poet. He wrote. . .

CURTAIN[33]

Furthermore, Marinetti denounced the unities of time, place and action and asserted the necessity for abolishing all conventions pertaining to the writing of dramatic literature. Although none of these pronouncements taken singly were innovative, the anti-Aristotelian aesthetic underlying Marinetti's vision went further than simply negating the established theatre of psychology, device and causal relationships in that it described an alternative, eclectic and energetic theatre. Furthermore, the degree to which the Futurists carried their program of renovation in both dramatic literature and performance techniques was innovative and consequential. The new manifesto called for an end to developmental, psychological, motivated characterization, preferring sparse, nonspecific characters similar to those depicted by the Symbolists and denoted as "he" or "women." These characters were sharp and streamlined, sometimes eliciting recognition of a type of person or class, as in the example just cited, but more often simply portraying "beings in action" which did not attempt to evoke complex responses based on empathy and character identity. By reducing and compressing identities, which also abolished certain facets of plot and entanglement associated with popular drama, the Futurists sheared away the excess verbiage from the theatre and opened the performance to original, spontaneous, simultaneous assortments of input from actors and audience, such as actor audience dialogue and improvisation.

Marinetti adhered emphatically to his earlier doctrine of entangling and involving the audience on as many levels as possible in the performance, and further, of provoking and encouraging the performance to continue on "into the street, the café, the morning after, the rest of one's life. . ." For, "Everything of any value is theatrical. . . . life itself . . . offers innumerable possibilities for the stage."[34] Marinetti believed that by intermingling actuality and performance the Futurist theatre would offer direct, concrete experience, an absolute antitheses to the vicarious illusion proffered by the theatre of realism, farce, melodrama or tragedy. The important Futurist principle of simultaneity was manifest in a theatre which could occur spontaneously in several areas of the auditorium and continue among diverse groups of people as they filtered out into the streets.

The intermingling of actuality and performance was often accomplished through devices which had little public exposure in established theatre.[35] The most effective method the Futurists used for engaging the audience was spontaneous actor-audience dialogue. These dialogues were probably effective because the audiences, in Milan especially, tended to be made up of a number of critics and artists who were known personally to the Futurists and possibly to other members of the audience.[36] The other effective device which the Futurists exploited was the structured and unstructured improvisation. The structured improvisation began with a scenario of activities and was carried to an agreed upon conclusion but was open to any interruption or digression which might occur from the audience. The unstructured improvisation apparently had no conclusion and only a brief description of activities to be included. Some of the 'sintesi' are believed to have been written after they had been performed as structured or unstructured improvisation. This speculation satisfies the wide margins of discrepancy between the written texts which are available for study and the descriptions from contemporary journals which assessed the same piece of material in performance.

Another technique for involving the spectator was subconscious as well as conscious involvement of the audience. This concept of cerebral stimulation had been translated from the "Painter's Manifesto" of 1911, discussed in section II of the present study. Just as the spectator standing in front of the Futurist canvas was stimulated to "become one with Being" and to "perceive the inner core of things," so the participant in the Futurist Theatre was bombarded with sensations which were aimed at opening new areas of awareness, pride and confidence. The Futurist Synthetic Theatre intended to distill and compress life itself, to synthesize the sensations "present for a moment in a tram, in a café, at a station, and which remain filmed on our minds as dynamic, fragmentary symphonies of gestures, words, noises, and lights."[37] The Futurist Synthetic Theatre used the same contemporary visual vocabulary which was at the foundation of Futurist painting (i.e., trains, trams, machines, physical activities, aeroplanes, guns, light). Moreover, this vocabulary was shaped in the Futurist Synthetic Theatre by the principle of simultaneity in much the same way that the painters had shaped this vocabulary in painting: where forms and lines had been overlapped and intermingled to explicate the interpenetration of objects and their reverberations, in Futurist painting overlapping and intermingling of activities, dialogue and ideas occurred in performance. One simple example, from Marinetti's play *The Communicating Vases,* written in 1916, demonstrates how the most rudimentary form of simultaneity operated on stage. Three different locations occupy the stage, in each of which the action goes on uninterrupted by or influenced by the actions of the other locations. Although the actions are fused at the end, they still have no logical relationship. Actors from one location break through the stage partitions into the other areas. Their action recalls the painter's device of force-lines, which were used to make visual the movement of objects in space and to describe their interpenetrability. The actions of these characters have no logical or sequential meaning: they simply obtrude into other compartments of the stage in the same sense that objects in Futurist paintings reverberate and interpenetrate with one another. In both cases the intention has been to stimulate the audience or spectator with various visual sensations (in the instance of performance, other auditory and tactile sensations could also be produced). Moreover, the simultaneous activities of the actors which overlap and interpenetrate because of the actual movement of bodies from one place to another described an event which was full of Futurist dynamism.[38] In the stage performance the actual movement of bodies and objects could be accomplished without the use of painterly symbols of movement through space. In this, the Futurist stage was closer to realizing the principle of dynamism than were the Futurist painters. The use of various illogical and unconnected stage actions such as dancing, juggling, hopping, jumping and others, reflect the translation of the principle of object movement, dynamism, which the painters were struggling with in such works as Boccioni's *States of Mind: Those Who Go,* which is pictured in Figure 5.

In a sintesi by Emilio Settimelli called *Passatism* the author used the device of nondevelopmental dialogue in a manner which clearly prefigures the use of this device by the writers associated with the Theatre of the Absurd, as well as earlier groups.

Passatism — by Settimelli

Act 1:

An old man and old woman are seated at a table, facing each other. Nearby is a calendar.

Man: How are you?
Woman: Not bad. And you?
Man: Not bad. (Pause). What a beautiful day tomorrow will be! (pause). Let's tear out the page, as usual: 10 January 1860. (pause). Did you have a good digestion?
Woman: Not bad.
Man: Did you overcome your dyspepsia?
Woman: I ate rather well and digested well. How happy I am!
Man: How happy I am! (Darkness)

Figure 5

Boccioni: Study for *States of Mind: Those Who Go* (1912).
(From *Futurism* [New York, Museum of Modern Art, 1961.)

Act 2:

Same scene, same arrangement.

Man: How are you?
Woman: Not bad. And you?
Man: Not bad. (pause). What a beautiful day tomorrow will be! (pause) Let's tear out the page as usual: 10 January 1880. (pause) Did you have a good digestion?
Woman: Not bad.
Man: Did you overcome your dyspepsia?
Woman: I ate rather well and digested well. How happy I am!
Man: How happy I am! (Darkness)

Act 3:

Same scene, same arrangement.

Man: How are you?
Woman: Not bad. And you?
Man: Not bad. (pause). What a beautiful day tomorrow will be! (pause) Let's tear out the page, as usual: 10 January 1910.
Woman: Oh, God! What a pain in the heart! I'm dying... (falls over and remains immobile).
Man: Oh, God! What a pain in the heart! I'm dying... (falls over and remains immobile).

CURTAIN

In this short and enigmatic piece, the questions raised are not answered. Who are these people? What is their raison d'etre? What is the author trying to do? Instead the audience is left with a visual image which involves the passage of time as symbolized by the calendar and the death of two people whose life had no apparent consequence. The dialogue contains none of the substance and information which would render a thematic idea intelligible to the audience. It simply repeats a series of commonplace exchanges which have no significance beyond that of everyday pleasantries.

Following the publication of the "Futurist Synthetic Theatre Manifesto," Marinetti and the Futurist playwrights and poets continued developing these principles. They wrote numerous 'sintesi' which were performed by travelling groups of actors and they reiterated in later manifestos the basic concepts and accomplishments of their theatre.

In 1915, as soon as Italy entered the war, Marinetti, Corrà, Balla, Russolo and Sant'Elia joined the Volunteer Cyclists. Boccioni joined the calvary. Communication between Marinetti and the members of the movement who were not engaged in the war was carried out by mail, telephone and telegraph. Although the movement kept up a stunning outpouring of publications, performances, and gallery shows throughout the war, Futurism underwent changes during and after the war years which can most logically be attributed to Marinetti's absence as a guiding force and to the changes in the movement's membership. In the areas of painting and sculpture these changes were fatal to the strength of the movement in Italy and abroad, as mentioned in Section II of this study.

In the development of Futurist theatre the changes which began in 1915 (after Marinetti's departure to the front) were both subtle and important in terms of the international reputation of the movement. Futurist theatre works had been primarily concerned with the relationship between the actor and the audience and with political and ideological ideas to be expressed by the actor. Moreover, the Futurists viewed their theatre as a political and philosophical arena where they could voice their programs in a variety of ways. The intellectual and entertainment possibilities of the theatre had been developed without the use of traditional scenography. Marinetti had defined the performance space as a continuation of the auditorium so that it more completely included both actors and spectators. The men who took over the leadership of the theater after Marinetti left had a different point of view.

The two men who found themselves in charge of the Futurist theatre in May 1915 were Enrico Prampolini (1894-1960) and Fortunato Depero (1892-1960). Both were accomplished painters who had been with the movement for several years, but whose main interest was directed toward the development of a Futurist scenography capable of expressing the complexities of modern life and celebrating the wonders of the technological age. In this their efforts were compatible with the general impulse of the "Foundation Manifesto" and manifestos which came after it. Prampolini and Depero began exploring the possibilities of mechanical scenography, thus moving away from the most basic concepts of "The Variety Theatre Manifesto" and "The Futurist Synthetic Theatre Manifesto." What had begun as a means of reforming the stage picture became instead a reform of the theatre itself.

The first manifesto addressed to the task of reforming scenography was written by Prampolini in 1915.

ENRICO PRAMPOLINI
Futurist Scenography
(April-May, 1915)

Let's reform the stage. To admit, to believe, that a stage exists today is to affirm that artistically man is absolutely blind. The stage is not equivalent to a photographic enlargement of a rectangle of reality or to a relative synthesis, but to the adoption of a theoretical and material system of subjective scenography completely opposed to the self-styled objective scenography of today.

It is not only a question of reforming the conception of the *mise-en-scene;* one must create an abstract entity that identifies with the scenic action of the play.

It is wrong to conceive of the stage separately, as a pictorial fact: (1) because now we are no longer dealing with scenography but with simple painting; (2) we are returning to the past (that is to say to the past. . . present) in which the stage expresses one subject, the play develops another. These two forces that have been diverging (playwright and scenographer) must converge so that a comprehensive synthesis of the play will result.

The stage must live the theatrical action in its dynamic synthesis; it must express the soul of the character conceived by the author just as the actor directly expresses and lives within himself.

Therefore, in order to reform the stage it is necessary to:

1. Refuse the exact reconstruction of what the playwright has conceived, thus definitely abandoning every real relationship, every comparison between object and subject and vice versa; all these relationships weaken direct emotion through indirect sensations.

2. Substitute for scenic action an emotional order that awakens all sensations necessary to the development of the work; the resulting atmosphere will provide the interior milieu.

3. Have *absolute synthesis* in material expression of the stage, that is to say, not the pictorial synthesis of all the elements, but synthesis excluding those elements of scenic architecture that are incapable of producing new sensations.

4. Make the scenic architecture be a connection for the audience's intuition rather than a picturesque and elaborate collaboration.

5. Have the colors and the stage arouse in the spectator those emotional values that neither the poet's words nor the actor's gestures can evoke.

There are no reformers of the stage today: Dresa and Rouché experimented in France with ingenious and infantile expressions; Meyerhold and Stanislavsky in Russia with revivals of nauseating classicism (we leave out the Assyrian-Persian-Egyptian-Nordic plagiarist Bakst); Adolphe Appia, Fritz Erler, Littman Fuchs, and Max Reinhardt (organizer) in Germany have attempted reforms directed more toward tedious elaboration, rich in glacial appearances, than toward the essential idea of interpretive reform: Granville-Barker and Gordon Craig in England have made some limited innovations, some objective syntheses.

Displays and material simplification, not rebellion against the past. It is this necessary revolution that we intend to provoke, because no one has had the artistic austerity to renovate the interpretive conception of the element to be expressed.

To us, scenography is a monstrous thing. Today's scenographers, sterile white-washers, still prowl around the dusty and stinking corners of classical architecture. We must rebel and assert ourselves and say to our poet and musician friends: this action demands this stage rather than that one.

Let us be artists too, and no longer merely executors. Let us create the stage, give life to the text with all the evocative power of our art. It is natural that we need plays suited to our sensibility, which imply a more intense and synthetic conception in the scenic development of subjects.

Let's renovate the stage. The absolutely new character that our innovation will give the theatre is *the abolition of the painted stage.* The stage will no longer be a colored backdrop but a *colorless electromechanical architecture, powerfully vitalized by chromatic emanations from a luminous source,* produced by electric reflectors with multicolored panes of glass, arranged, coordinated analogically with the psyche of each scenic action.

With the luminous irradiations of these beams, of these planes of colored lights, the dynamic combinations will give marvelous results of mutual permeation, of intersection of lights and shadows. From these will arise vacant abandonments, exultant, luminous corporalities.

These assemblages, these unreal shocks, this exuberance of sensations combined with dynamic stage architecture that will move, unleashing metallic arms, knocking over plastic planes, amidst an essentially new modern noise, will augment the vital intensity of the scenic action.

On a stage illuminated in such a way, the actors will gain unexpected dynamic effects that are neglected or very seldom employed in today's theatres, mostly because of the ancient prejudice that one must imitate, represent reality.

And with what purpose?

Perhaps scenographers believe it is absolutely necessary to represent this reality? Idiots! Don't you understand that your efforts, your useless realistic preoccupations have no effect other than that of diminishing the intensity and emotional content, which can be attained precisely through the interpretive equivalents of these realities, i.e., abstractions?

Let's create the stage. In the above lines we have upheld the idea of a *dynamic stage* as opposed to the static stage of another time; with the fundamental principles that we shall set forth, we intend not only to carry the stage to its most advanced expression but also to attribute to it the essential values that belong to it and that no one has thought of giving it until now.

Let's reverse the roles. Instead of the illuminated stage, let's create the *illuminating stage: luminous expression that will irradiate the colors demanded by the theatrical action with all its emotional power.*

The material means of expressing this illuminating stage consist in the use of electrochemical colors, fluorescent mixtures that have the chemical property of being susceptible to electric currents and diffusing luminous colorations of all tonalities according to the combinations of fluorine and other mixtures of gases. The desired effects of exciting luminosity will be obtained with electric neon (ultraviolet) tubes, systematically arranging these mixtures according to an agreed-upon design in this immense scenodynamic architecture. But the Futurist scenographic and choreographic evolution must not stop there. In the final synthesis, human actors will no longer be tolerated, like children's marionettes or today's supermarionettes recommended by recent reformers; neither one nor the other can sufficiently express the multiple aspects conceived by the playwright.

In the totally realizable epoch of Futurism we shall see the luminous dynamic architectures of the stage emanate from chromatic incandescences that, climbing tragically or showing themselves voluptuously, will inevitably arouse new sensations and emotional values in the spectator.

Vibrations, luminous forms (produced by electric currents and colored gases) will wriggle and writhe dynamically, and these authentic actor-gases of an unknown theatre will have to replace living actors. By shrill whistles and strange noises these actor-gases will be able to give the unusual significations of theatrical interpretations quite well; they will be able to express these multiform emotive tonalities with much more effectiveness than some celebrated actor or other can with his displays. These exhilarant, explosive gases will fill the audience with joy or terror, and the audience will perhaps become an actor itself as well.

But these words are not our last. We still have much more to say. First let's carry out what we have set forth above.

Prampolini's manifesto, written four months after the "Futurist Synthetic Theatre Manifesto," was clear and concise in outlining the nature of the new Futurist stage. However, in tone and spirit it was unlike the other manifestos. Moreover, it was not primarily concerned with the same aims which Marinetti set forth for the movement. There was no war rhetoric, no appeals for the revelation of man's inner core. Prampolini was more preoccupied with elevating his profession and bringing new values to scenography; Futurist devices served that purpose. Due to the works of Prampolini and Depero, the innovations made in stage decor between 1916 and 1929 have been regarded by most historians as the seminal contributions of Futurist Theatre.

Essentially, Prampolini suggested five central concepts. The stage picture was to become part of the stage action, no longer a static passive background against which stage action occurred. Therefore, the stage space would become an important concern of the theatre producer instead of being largely ignored in favor of the actor. The space was envisioned as having dynamic potential; that is, technological progress had provided the scenographer with the means to produce illuminations electrically which could be used to fill the stage space. These illuminations in conjunction with gases, both of which were possible in a variety of colors, would "interact and compenetrate" in endless combinations which would stir the audience with new electric sensations. Finally, the dynamic stage would render the actor unnecessary.

The elimination of the actor from the stage was in contradiction to the principles which Marinetti had developed in his theatre manifestos. Moreover, these two hypotheses could not be resolved without compromise. Evidence suggests that due to the financial and practical difficulties of constructing the theatre space Prampolini described, any conflict of interest was avoided and dissolved over the decade between 1916-1926. Although both Prampolini and Depero continued to publish documents advertizing and restating their ideas for a mechanized theatre space, the designs which they rendered for Futurist performances usually achieved a compromise. Using the vocabularies of Cubism and Futurism, they developed geometricality as the dominant aspect of their designs. The modification of the performer to this geometry complemented the design. For example, Prampolini designed a set for a 'sintesi' by Buzzi called *Parallelepiped* in 1921. The set, pictured in Figure 6, while it convincingly utilizes variations of cubic forms to define and modify the acting space, does not produce "electrochemical architecture, powerfully vitalized by chromatic emanations from a luminous source."[39] Nevertheless, in 1921 Prampolini's

Figure 6

Prampolini set design for *Parallelepiped* by Buzzi (1921).
(From *Futurist Performance* by Michael Kirby
[New York: E.P. Dutton and Co., Inc., 1971].)

design was indicative of the work of an innovative group of scenographers who had moved away from the prevalent styles of naturalism and symbolism. Prampolini has separated the forestage and backstage by using the act curtain in a straightforward manner which makes no pretence of being illusory. His free-standing geometric constructions suggested instability, a lack of equilibrium and confusion of depth. Moreover, Prampolini broke up the acting space in a subtle manner by creating illogical spatial relationships between actors and set. By running his orthagonal axes against the traditional perspective, he achieved a startling conflict between the upstage and downstage heights of set and performer.

The most obvious manifestation of the compromise between an automated and a live theatre occurred in the area of Futurist costume design. In a document dated 1915 Depero described the mechanical costume-type which was subsequently utilized in numerous forms in Futurist performance.

Depero: Description of Costumes (1915)

Apparition-like costume equivalent (magical, mechanical) to *complex simultaneity of forms – colors – onomatopoeia – sounds and noises.* Constructed on a framework of metallic wire – light – forms of transparent material – brightly colored.

The framework will be made so as to open and close itself, that is to say, it must appear like a normal Futurist costume but the jacket opens by clicking one's heels; various movements with one's arms, hands, feet, legs, or raising one's hat, etc. . . will open certain fanlike contrivances like tongs, etc. . . .simultaneously with luminous Apparitions in bursts and rhythms of noiselike instruments.

The costumes for the Futurist abstract and dynamic theatre to come will be constructed on this very new principle of Depero's that was inaugurated by Marinetti at the extraordinary Depero-Balla Exposition of 1915.[40] (See Figure 7)

The mechanical costume was original and the characteristic humor and extravagance of Depero's idea were particularly Futurist. Futurist humor, despite the overbearing tone of many Futurist publications, was consistently noted for its raucousness and true spontaneity.

Following the publication of Prampolini's manifesto in 1915, "Notes on the Theatre" by Depero appeared in the Italian press between 1915 and 1917. Although he echoed some of Prampolini's concepts, Depero introduced new devices to be used in Futurist scenography.

Notes on the Theatre – Depero[41]

Not only must every event, act, and phenomenon be represented by lines, colors, forms, environments, and costumes of renewed style, but movement also must be a vast re-creation of mimicry.

Every displacement of an object or figure, every thought, dream, intention, and vision will be mimetically in direct relationship to the environment: also mimicry

Figure 7

Plastic costume for *Mimismagia* (mimetic magic), 1916, by Depero.
(From *Depero* catalogue by Bruno Passamani
[Roverero: Bassano de Grappa Museo Civico, 1970].)

will be the only scenario in some cases; e.g., turning flowers, moving mountains, trees and steeples that oscillate, houses that uncover and open themselves; wind that tosses, shakes, drops, and overturns the landscape with whirlwinds, while, in a tragic fixity, characters remain immobile. A single figure, too, can become the protagonist of plastic-magic phenomena: enlargement of the eyes and various illuminations of them. Decompositions of the figure and the deformation of it, even until its absolute transformation; e.g., a dancing ballerina who continually accelerates, transforming herself into a floral vortex, etc.

Also, the construction of the stage must be completely redone and amplified in all electrical and mechanical senses. The stage must be ready and prepared for all possibilities, in order that every intention of the artist can be rendered feasible.

Appearances at the sides on a fixed horizontal floor are not enough, nor are the usual lowerings from the ceiling; but every side including the floor, indeed the floor itself, will be raised and the scenes will be seen in their vast topography, or the floors will be multiplied and the characters will be at disproportionate perspectives, etc.

Mobile Scenery. The complex *motorumorista*[42] suggested to me mobile scenery and transformation. The sun appears and disappears every day. The clouds pass, men and animals walk. Machines wind, rotate, and pull; toothed, geared, complicated, and simple.

Cycles, motors, autos, running noisily or silently, in gusts, in darts. Trains with nostril-tubes puff carelessly, bullets flashing-threads, fish rolling-lights in water, birds fluttering-mastiffs of the air.

The luxurious autos in the squares and on the black, glossy rubber boulevards create snares of lights and phosphorescent bolas that, thrown by invisible gauchos, ensnare the fleeing taxis red-devil-bats.

Everything turns-disappears-reappears, multiplies and breaks, pulverizes and overturns, trembles and transforms into a cosmic machine that is life. And theatre?

The wings may turn on their own flashing-arc, the backcloths may turn on changeable multipivots. Pieces of furniture may flee and may fight one another, or, rallied, may hunt the tenants; oil lanterns and electric lamps may clash, bombarding each other, or may foxtrot on the backcloth or in the madness of the crowd; sensational news and dramatic situations may create typographic scenery, those luminous advertising walls, originating sonorously in all timbres from megaphones of the heart and the soul.

The theatre must interpret, synthesize, infinitely re-create all the *visual-auditory-olfactory-dramatic-electric-hypnotic and magic* round dances of our life.

Life is lived speedily. Theatre errs through slowness.

Why does cinematography triumph? In spite of lacking color, constructions, and relief, voices and living characters!

And still a simple succession of black-and-white photographs! It wins because it is fast, because it moves and transforms rapidly. Cinematography is varied and rich, improvised, and surprising.

> *. . . a hand that robs*
> *. . . two others than turn a wheel*
> *. . . a forest that flies*

... a palace that collapses
... a tunnel that sucks itself up
... a steamer that lies on the sea
... a New York street with congested traffic
... and the solitary banks of a river

One runs, navigates, flies, takes a voyage, lives intensely, while resting comfortably seated in an armchair.

Cinematography, removed from the assassin's hands of certain reconstructors of historical dramas, perfectly fake and useless, and of melancholy makers of banal human passions who wish to bring it back to the boring idiocies of the theatre, will become a powerful means of artistic creation.

It is necessary to add to theatre everything that is suggested by cinematography.

Depero's "Notes" expressed a fundamental preoccupation with the cinema which absorbed most of the Futurists. Distinctions between stage and film were seen only in the speed with which film could impress the spectator with sensations, and in the film, the Futurists admired the potential for simultaneity, variety and surprise—all three concepts of the utmost importance. Hence, film was immediately perceived as a "powerful means of artistic creation . . . it is necessary to add to theatre everything that is suggested by cinematography." The Futurists were among the first theatre workers to contend with the new media, film, which was so obviously related to theatre but also in competition with it. Their enthusiastic incorporation of cinematic techniques and cinema itself into the vocabulary of the stage fostered a period of healthy interaction between the two performance forms. However, Depero clearly recognized the growing popularity of film posed a threat to the survival of the theatre. The Futurists chose to imitate and outdo the film; an objective which has proven unattainable.

The other central proposition of Depero's "Notes" concerned movable scenery. Movable scenery was a further development of Prampolini's concept of "electrochemical architecture" with a more practical application. Depero envisioned a stage with its typical accoutrements capable of a variety of movements to create an active stage space. Among his examples of the mechanized stage scene he mentions "Sensational news and dramatic situations may create typographic scenery, those luminous advertising walls. . . ." The use of multiple media or "mixed media" was inherent in the use of the typographic revolution in literature and in Balla's set for *Printing Press.* Once the potential for incorporating letters and words into non-literary forms was introduced, the translation of that device into a usable scenographic form was inevitable for the Futurists. The use of several types of visual communication used in conjunction was another manifestation of the principle of simultaneity, one which was later employed by other avant garde theatre groups.

The earliest production to accomplish many of Prampolini's and Depero's most revolutionary goals was designed and executed by Balla in 1917 for Serge Diaghilev's Ballet Russes. In this production, *Feu d'Artifice,* most of the major concepts articulated by Depero and Prampolini were realized in a production which astounded and delighted audiences first in Rome and later in Paris. Michael Kirby, who has studied many of the original drawings and spoken with persons who were connected with the Futurists in Italy, gives an excellent account of Balla's design in his book *Futurist Performance:*

> Thus one of the most significant and prophetic of all Futurist performances was Giacoma Balla's staging of Stravinsky's *Fireworks (Feu d'Artifice)* for Diaghilev's Ballet Russe at the Costanzi Theatre in Rome on April 12, 1917. Although it can be said that Balla "staged" the piece, Stravinsky's work was not a play, opera, or ballet; it had no story or characters and was merely a musical composition. For it Balla created a performance without actors in which the dynamics of light were of primary importance.
>
> Balla filled the stage with what might best be described as a tremendously enlarged three-dimensional version of one of his non-objective paintings. Irregular prismatic forms jutted up at various angles to different heights above the stage floor. These solid forms were made of wood; Balla's working drawings for their construction still exist (Figure 8). They were then covered with cloth and painted. On top of most of these large irregular shapes were smaller forms covered with translucent fabric and painted with brightly colored zigzags, rays, and bars. These smaller forms, which occupied the central areas of the stage composition, could be illuminated from inside. The entire grouping of shapes was displayed against a black background.
>
> Balla built a "keyboard" of switches in the prompter's box, so that he could watch and listen to the performance while he "played" the lights. His notes for the operation of the lights indicate forty-nine different settings, but, since some passages were repeated, there were actually more than that number of changes in the illumination. The performance, which was conducted by Ansermet, lasted five minutes. Thus, coordinated with the music, there was a change in the lighting about every five seconds, on the average. Lighting possibilities included various combinations of external illumination on the solid forms, internal illumination of the translucent shapes and illumination of the black backdrop, which once was colored with rays of red light. Shadows also played a part in Balla's lighting design, and two of the cues on his plot indicate shadow projectors. It was not merely the stage that was lit, however: the auditorium itself was illuminated and darkened during the piece, relating the spectators to the actorless presentation on stage. In *Fireworks,* sound, light and color were orchestrated into a single, entirely nonrepresentational work.[43] (Figure 9)

In 1918 Marinetti returned from the front lines. The war in Italy was over except for the signing of the final documents. Among the changes that awaited him in Milan, the change in the political climate of Italy was the greatest. The Russian Revolution had begun; its impact on Italy was enormous. The battle for control was well underway in 1918 and Marinetti lost no time

Figure 8

Balla's working sketch for basic stage unit of Feu d'Artifice, 1917.
(From *Futurist Performance* by Michael Kirby
[New York: E.P. Dutton and Co., Inc., 1971].)

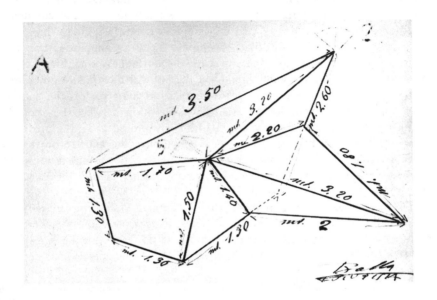

choosing sides. He had been a friend of Benito Mussolini, the young pacifist journalist, now the leader of the Italian Fasceti, who had finally renounced his Socialist friends and joined the nationalists and Futurists in 1915, and it was with Mussolini that Marinetti allied himself.

Mussolini was shrewd and calculating in his use of his friend Marinetti. During the next six years, while Il Duce was establishing and then stabilizing his control, Marinetti performed innumerable services for him and conducted many successful campaigns to swing the people over to Mussolini's camp. After his success was ensured, Mussolini repaid his friend by appointing him to a meaningless bureaucratic job and mocking the buffoonery and brashness of Marinetti's campaign. Mussolini supported the Futurist theatre and other areas of the movement, however, by regarding them as more or less the national voice of the government in the arts. The association between Fascism and Futurism in the minds of many critics ultimately proved to be the proverbial "kiss of death" for the Futurist movement, although the alliance proved fortuitous in one respect. Through Mussolini's support, the Futurists were able to build an ambitious Experimental Theatre, which included the most impressive mechanical devices available anywhere (pictured in Figure 10). This marvelous theatre was located in the Baths of Septimus Severus, a dungeon-like cellar under Mussolini's home in Rome. *Theatre Magazine* had a representative in Rome who regularly attended productions at the Experimental Theatre in 1924-25. Maxim Gordon described the theatre in the September 1925 issue:

> In the cellar of the Palazzo Titoni, the modern home of Mussolini, there were still to be seen a few years back the ruins of the Baths of Septimus Severus. It was this highly connotative, if dilapidated, interior which the Futurists took for their Teatro Sperimentale and the Casa d'Arte, run by Anton Bragaglia in connection with the theatre. The transformation is at once magical and ironic. In place of the crumbling masonry and debris which remained as relics of the ante-Christian era, we now find symmetrical columns and arches, twisted iron scrolls, fantastic lamps, non-representative paintings and cubistic furniture. The theatre, the gallery and the adjoining restaurant present an unusual arrangement of unexpected angles and curious curves, an interior as far removed as possible from any suggestion of the past.[44]

That same year, while the Futurists were entertaining an international public in their theatre in Rome, Prampolini was awarded the first prize for stage design at the International Exposition of Decorative Arts in Paris. His entry was financed by the government, and was an elaborate mechanical model of the Magnetic Theatre.

The Magnetic Theatre was a complicated construction of wheels, platforms, geometric solids, spheres and wires which were to "replace the actors as focus for the performance." Prampolini described the Magnetic Theatre in 1926. The structure was:

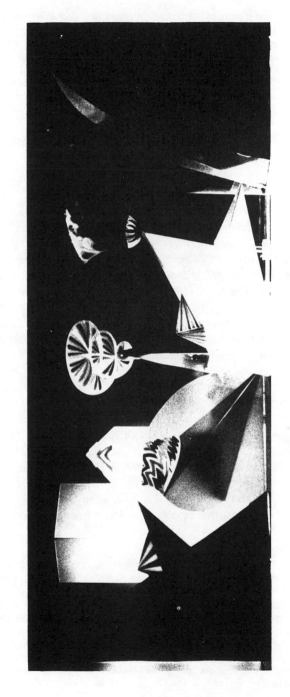

Figure 9

Photograph of a reconstruction of Balla's set for *Fireworks*, 1917. Reconstruction by Elio Marcheqiana. (From catalogue of the show *Depero*, Galleria l'Obelisco, Rome, 1969.)

. . . made up of a mass of plastic constructions in action which rises from the centre of the theatrical hollow instead of the periphery of the "scenic-arc." Auxiliary moving constructions rise, first on a square movable platform, standing on an elevator. On this in turn is erected a *moving, rolling platform* going in the opposite direction from the first, and likewise carrying other *planes* and *auxiliary volumes.* To these plastic constructions, *ascending, rotating* and *shifting* movements are given, in accordance with necessity. The scenic action of the chromatic light, an essential element of interaction in creating the scenic personality of space, unfolds parallel to the scenic development of these moving constructions. Its function is to give *spiritual life* to the environment or setting, while measuring time in *scenic space.* This chromatic ladder will be made with apparatuses of *projection, refraction, and diffusion.* [45]

The Magnetic Theatre (Figure 11) was a completely abstract machine which would use space and mass, movement, light and sound to create a performance. The performance created by the shifting and moving light which fell upon the parts of the machine was supposed to restore a "spiritual virginity to scenic matter." With the Magnetic Theatre Prampolini brought to a culmination the ideas which he had articulated with Depero and Balla in 1915.

The Magnetic Theatre Machine demonstrated the contradictions between two distinct viewpoints. Prampolini and Depero created machinery which permitted the audience to move around the outside of a performance, on an ambulatory, but which permitted no interaction between audience and event. This procedure was in contrast to Marinetti, who had argued that the audience and event must be integrated.

Marinetti reasserted his original position in his final theatre-related manifesto, "The Total Theatre Manifesto," which he published after retiring from the government position he held. The "Total Theatre Manifesto" of 1933 was perhaps his most intriguing and profound vision. Furthermore, evidence suggests that it was his last major contribution until his death in 1944.

In the "Total Theatre Manifesto" Marinetti pulls together the two major facets of the Futurist theatre into a single, cohesive statement which was to include every aspect and every possibility which had been suggested over the last twenty years. Here was the resolution of architecture, machine, actor and audience.

The fixed or revolving stage of the contemporary theatre is more or less comparable to a little theatre for children. It is more suited to marionettes than to live actors. It is reminiscent of the fireplaces of Medieval castles or, rather, to an aviary, the inmates being imprisoned by backdrop and sidewings while the interior part of the structure gives only the illusion of freedom. We Futurists have idealized a Total Theatre accompanied by an extremely original architectural structure. There have been many such structures but always too moderately conceived and insufficient in correcting the monotony of single scene to single action relationship. There is a need to boldly free the spectator from his submissive and servile immobility and put him in motion.

Figure 10

"The Living Plastic Ensemble," a hypothetical plan for a movable stage
designed by Depero for the Experimental Theatre 1924.
(From *Depero e la scena da "Colori,, alla scena mobile 1916-1930*
by Passamani.)

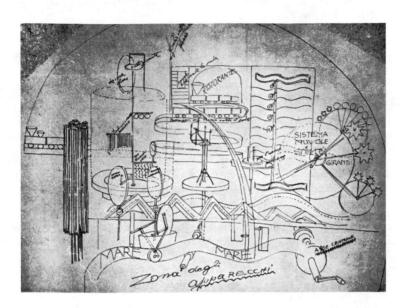

For twenty three years we have advocated the law of simultaneity in theatre art which condemns the concept of the single scene and states that each episode in life has an infinite number of episodes relative and contemporaneous to it, of either a conflicting or favorable nature which serve to enrich it in meaning and drama.

We propose to circle the spectators around many circular stages on which several diverse actions are unfolding simultaneously within a vast spectrum of graduated intensities. This will be enhanced by a corroborating organization of cinematography, radiophony, telephone, electric lights, neon lights, aerial painting, aerial poetry, tactilism, humor and smells.

ARCHITECTURE and MECHANISM of the TOTAL THEATRE (Synthetic, poly-sensational, simultaneous, polyscenic, aerial pictorial, aerial poetic, cinematographic, radiophonic, olfactory, tactile and noisy.)

The theatre is to be constructed according to the great principles of the Futurist Sant 'Elia, father of the new architecture. It is a round diameter of 200 meters. An apron stage runs circular to the interior wall. This apron is 2 meters high, 10 meters wide and 5 meters from the interior wall. The walls themselves are slightly curved so that they can be used for cinematography, television, aerial pictures and aerial poetic projections. Under the circular apron there is a mote that forms a large ring of water circumscribing the stage proper. (Sea or river, waterfalls, dives, boat races, suicides, effects of underwater life, multiplication of reflections.)

In the center of the main stage there are eleven round stages without wings around which each spectator moves in his circulating table-chair. In his table-chair he can follow with successive velocity the diverse actions of the various stages which intercommunicate with each other underground. On the walkway which around the eleven stages along the moat, the spectator, in groups or individually, can them-selves unfold capricious adventures of a journey, participating in the nautical actions going on in the moat. Or, they can disappear by elevator to the bright underground levels for refreshments and rest.

The spectators, having participated as actors reciting and communicating to each other by way of their radio-telephones like dispersed army troops, can each return to his revolving table-chair. Close at hand on each of these table-chairs there is a tape which rapidly transmits to each spectator unexpected tactile sensations which are tempered by or accentuated by odors. These odors are controlled by a keyboard and each odor is successively cancelled by special aspirators or vacuum cleaners. For example, the spectator can enjoy a fantastic student revellry six meters away, or the idyllic pleasure of many kisses under the dark canopy on the right, or a furious jealous fray between a married couple fifty meters away, or the rescue of a stubborn suicide attempt ten meters below him, or an aerial pictorial or an aerial battle by Enrico Prampolini on the high wall before him while the hurricane of colors repre-senting one of the festivals of Depero forces him to turn to the screen on his left where a parade of march and drill teams invade the screen. At intervals the hidden music of orchestras and choruses floats out through the floor. Opportune periods of silence lasting seven or eight seconds will allow the necessary rearrangement of thoughts for the agitated spectator's mind. The emotional crescendo of the various spectacles culminates on the large round stage where the light at the zenith of the cupola is a celestial heavens of the theatre which shows a mechanical dramatization of the movement of the sun, moon, constellations, aeroplanes with colored smoke. Thus the rays of an enormous red globe, a magnificent sunrise, floods the spectators.

Figure 11

Prampolini's drawing of his Magnetic Theatre.
(Courtesy of Dr. Alessandro Prampolini; from a reproduction in
Futurist Performance by Michael Kirby
[New York: E.P. Dutton and Co., 1971].)

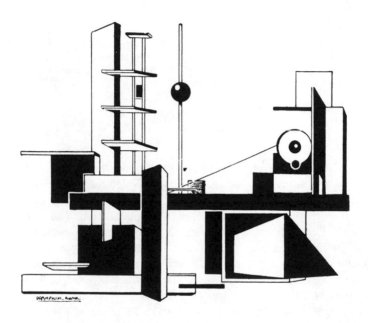

Then, if need be, it changes to a vermillion sunset slightly toned by the icy pallor of the rising moonlight. This becomes immersed with the perspectives of a crowded American city street transmitted by way of television. At a lower level the realism of a film showing a big game hunt complete with rifle shots is offset by a projection of a purely abstract representation of an aerial pictorial by Balla, Benedotta, Dottori o Di fillia. The spectator is thus enjoyably immersed in contrasting luminous atmospheres. The unity which dominates the actions of the various stages, screens and celestial orbits is broken by the creative, improvised outbursts from the spectators and occasionally by an intentional breakdown in the communication system between the stages. Thus it attains new effects either humorous or tragic in the general aerial pictorial drama as well as in the terrestrial marine fluvial drama.

The Total Theatre can thus synthesize all the forces of a worldwide Futurism from the typical creations of a plastic dynamism, revolutionizing our times, to the turbulent life of the great American urban centers; from the beautiful aerial paintings and aerial poetry, introduced recently by the magazine *Futurism* to the delightful explosion of the futuristic spectators.

The past does not exist.
Demilitarized boredom is defeated.
Hooray for the Total Theatre.[46]

The Futurist movement had an impact on nearly every development of modern art, directly or indirectly, and provided an important stimulus to the writing, staging and design of drama. Translations of the "Synthetic Theatre Manifesto" appeared within eight weeks of its publication. The activities which began with Futurism were incorporated with many interesting and consequential modifications into every major theatre experiment of this century. Marinetti and others of the movement travelled extensively, speaking, debating and presenting Futurist ideas in the artistic centers of Europe. The well documented trips to Russia and England in 1913-14 were two which had particularly interesting results in the formation of Russian Futurism and the English movement Vorticism.

In Zurich, the Dadaists capitalized on most of the pre-war Futurist proposals and techniques in launching their movement. Many of the Surrealists have asserted the primacy of Futurism as an influence on their development. In Germany, the Bauhaus' collaboration was demonstrably cognizant of and intrigued by many of the Futurists' activities and publications. In this country, the Living Newspaper technique of the Thirties was an adaptation of Marinetti's Total Theatre concept which advocated projecting "startling or important newspaper headlines" around a circular auditorium. Thorton Wilder was present at a number of Futurist performances in 1921 from which he drew the seminal concepts which are visually identifiable in his plays.

More recently, fisificolla-bodymadness has erupted in numerous artistic manifestations from Jackson Pollack's "Action Painting" to the action built into the Happenings and Events of the early 1960's.

Ideas and theories which described a total theatre have been articulated since Aristotle. The accomplishment of Futurism was to update the vocabularies of all the arts to meet the demands of the twentieth century. The Futurists pulled the boundaries of each discipline out of shape and overlapped them, one upon another, causing a stimulating flow of ideas among artists. They observed no rules or conventions except the rule of moving ahead, of never being satisfied with what they had done. They were, often, unable to produce a satisfactory synthesis of theory and practice. Nevertheless, in most of their endeavors they were far ahead of the rest of the world, at least theoretically. Indeed, we have not yet seen the end of the explorations which their work suggested in painting, architecture, theatre, music, film or literature. Perhaps their most important legacy was their gift for serious commitment combined with an eloquent sense of the bizarre which has impregnated the arts of the twentieth century.

APPENDIX A

The Antineutral Dress
Giacomo Balla
1915

Humanity has always dressed itself in *quiet,* in *fear,* in *caution* or in *indecision,* it has always worn mourning, disappointment or the cloak. The human body has always been diminished *neutral* shades and tints, afflicted by black, suffocated by belts, imprisoned by clothing.

Until today men have worn clothes of static colors and styles, that is draped, solemn, grave, uncomfortable and priestly. They expressed timidity, melancholy and slavery, a negation of the muscular life, suffocating in an unhygienic "passatism" of heavy materials and tedious tints, effeminate or decadent. Tonality and rhythms of a desolate peace, funereal and depressing.

Today we want to abolish:

1. All neutral tints, "cute," faded, printed, semi-dark and humiliating.
2. All tints and patterns (or styles) which are pedantic, professorial and teutonic. Designs of lines, checks (squares) or pin stripes.
3. Mourning clothes, which are not even suitable for undertakers. Heroic deaths should not be mourned, but remembered by red clothing.
4. Mediocracy, the so called good taste and the so called harmony of tints and styles, which restrain enthusiasm and slow down the pace (or step).
5. The symmetry of the cut, the static lines which tire, depress, restrain, tie the muscles; the uniformity of bulky cuffs and all the trappings. The useless buttons. Starched collars and cuffs.

We futurists want to liberate our race from all neutrality, from the fearful and quiet indecision, from the negative pessimism and from nostalgic romantic and softening inertia. We want to color Italy with audacity and futurist risk, to finally endow Italians with bellicose and gay clothing.

Futurist clothes, then, will be:

1. Aggressive to such an extent as to multiply the courage of the brave and upset the sensibility of the vile (people, that is).
2. Agile, that is, capable of increasing the flexibility of the body and give impetus (or more freedom) in the act of battle or in walking or running.
3. Dynamic in design and colors, dynamic in the prints (triangles, cones, spirals, ellipses, circles) to inspire love of danger, velocity and aggressiveness, the hatred of peace and immobility.
4. Simple and comfortable, that is easy to get on and off, suitable for firing a rifle, crossing a stream or swimming.
5. Hygienic, that is cut and styled in such a way that each part of the skin may breathe freely during long marches and tiring climbs.

6. Gay. Materials of such colors and irridescences as to inspire enthusiasm. Utilize *muscular* colors of the brightest shades of violet, red, turquoise, yellow, green, orange, vermillion.

7. Luminous. Phosphorescent materials to ignite temerity in an assembly of fearful people, spread brightness when it rains and to rebuke the greyness of twilight in both the streets and on the nerves.

8. Volitive. Violent colors and designs, imperious and impetuous like battlefield orders.

9. Asymmetrical. For instance, the edges of the sleeves and of the jacket front will be cut round on the right side, square on the left side. Ingenious counterattacks of lines.

10. The clothes will not be made to last a long time in order to constantly renew the pleasure and impetuous animation of the body.

11. Variable, by means of *modifiers* (appliqués of various materials, widths, thicknesses, designs and colors) to be arranged when and where one wishes on various parts of the dress by means of pneumatic buttons. Thus, anyone can invent a new dress at any time. The modifier is to be overwhelming, shocking, clashing, decisive, war-like, etc.

The futurist hat will be asymmetrical, of aggressive and merry colors. Futurist shoes will be dynamic, one different from the other in style and color, suitable for cheerfully kicking all "neutralists."

The combination of yellow and black will be brutally excluded.

One thinks and acts according to how one dresses. Since neutrality is the synthesis of all passeists, today we futurists will brandish these antineutral clothes, cheerfully bellicose.

Only the "podagrosi"* will disapprove of us.

The youth of Italy will recognize in us, who wear these clothes, its futurist living flags for our great, necessary, urgent war.

If the government will not depose its passéist dress of fear and indecision, we will double, centuplicate (100) the red of the tricolor which we wear.

Figure 12

Manifesto on antineutral dress with illustrations by Giacomo Balla, 1914
(From *Metro, The International Review of Contemporary Art*
[San Marco: Alfiere, 1970] .)

IL VESTITO ANTINEUTRALE

Manifesto futurista

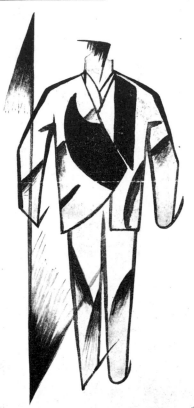

**Glorifichiamo la guerra,
sola igiene del mondo.**
MARINETTI.
(I° Manifesto del Futurismo - 20 Febbraio 1909)

Viva Asinari di Bernezzo !
MARINETTI.
(I° Serata futurista - Teatro Lirico, Milano, Febbraio 1910)

L'umanità si vestì sempre di **quiete**, di **paura**, di **cautela** o d'**indecisione**, portò sempre il lutto, o il piviale, o il mantello. Il corpo dell'uomo fu sempre diminuito da sfumature e da tinte **neutre**, avvilito dal nero, soffocato da cinture, imprigionato da panneggiamenti.

Fino ad oggi gli uomini usarono abiti di colori o forme statiche, cioè drappeggiati, solenni, gravi, incomodi e sacerdotali. Erano espressioni di timidezza, di malinconia e di **schiavitù**, negazione della vita muscolare, che soffocava in un passatismo anti-igienico di stoffe troppo pesanti e di mezze tinte tediose, effeminate o decadenti. Tonalità e ritmi di **pace desolante**, funeraria e deprimente.
OGGI vogliamo abolire:
1. — Tutte le tinte **neutre**, « carine », sbiadite, *fantasia*, semioscure e umilianti.
2. — Tutte le tinte e le foggie pedanti, professorali e teutoniche. I disegni a righe, a quadretti, a **puntini diplomatici.**
3. — I vestiti da lutto, nemmeno adatti per i becchini. Le morti eroiche non devono essere compiante, ma ricordate con vestiti rossi.
4. — L'equilibrio **mediocrista**, il cosidetto buon gusto e la cosidetta armonia di tinte e di forme, che frenano gli entusiasmi e rallentano il passo.
5. — La simmetria nel taglio, le linee **statiche**, che stancano, deprimono, contristano, legano i muscoli; l'uniformità di goffi risvolti e tutte le cincischiature. I bottoni inutili. I colletti e i polsini inamidati.

Noi futuristi vogliamo liberare la nostra razza da ogni **neutralità**, dall'indecisione paurosa e quietista, dal pessimismo negatore e dall'inerzia

Vestito bianco - rosso - verde
del parolibero futurista Marinetti. *(Mattino)*

APPENDIX B

The Surprise Theatre
by Filippo Tommaso Marinetti and Francesca Cangiullo
1921

Futurism
Synthetic, illustrated magazine

We have renewed and glorified the Variety Theatre. In the Synthetic Theatre we have destroyed the worries of technique, verisimilitude, logical continuation and gradual preparation.

We have created in the Synthetic Theatre the new mixtures of serious and comic, of real and unreal personages, penetration and simultaneity of time and space, dramas of objects, dissonances, staged images, the showcases of ideas and gestures. If there exists today a young Italian theatre with a blend of the serio-comic-grotesque, unreal personages in unreal ambients, simultaneity and penetration of time and space, it is due to our Synthetic Theatre.

Today we impose on the theatre another jump forward. Our Theatre of Surprise proposes to exhilarate by surprising through contrasting methods, facts, ideas which have not as yet introduced to the stage, entertaining conglomerations which have not as yet taken advantage of but capable of cheerfully shaking human sensibility.

We have often stated that surprise is the essential element of art, that the work of art is autonomous, it resembles only itself and therefore appears as a prodigy. In fact, The Spring by Botticelli – like many other masterpieces – had at its appearance, other than the various elements of composition, rhythms, mass and colors the essential value of its surprising originality. A familiarity with this painting, the imitations that it inspired have destroyed this value of originality. This demonstrates how the cult for past works (admired, imitated, and plagiarized) is, aside from pernicious to new geniuses, vain and absurd since today we can only admire, imitate and plagiarize only a part of these works.

Raphael, having chosen for one of his frescos a wall in a room in the Vatican which had already been decorated the year before by Sodoma, effaced the marvelous work of that painter and repainted it, in homage to his own creative pride, thinking that the principal value of a work of art consists in its surprising apparition.

Therefore we give absolute importance to the value of surprise. Especially after so many centuries of ingenious works which (upon the appearance of each) surprised, today it is difficult to surprise.

In the Theatre of Surprise, the "innovative rock" which the author launches must be such as to:

1. Hit with merry surprise the sensibility of the public in full.

2. Suggest a wave of other extremely humorous ideas, like so many concentric circles or echoes.

3. Provoke in the public words and actions which are totally unexpected, so that one surprise will evoke new surprises in the theatre, in the city that very same night, the next day, ad infinitum.

By training the Italian spirit to its utmost elasticity, with all its extra-logical spiritual gymnastics The Theatre of Surprise wants to tear the youth of Italy away from the monotonous, funereal, stupefying political obsession.

81

To conclude: The Theatre of Surprise contains, other than the physical-follies of a concert hall with participating gymnasts, athletes, magicians, eccentrics, jugglers, other than the Synthetic Theatre, also a Theatre-newspaper of the futurist movement and a plastic theatre-gallery as well as dynamic declamations and presentations of "free-words," dances staged free-word poems, improv musical discussions between pianos, between pianos and songs, free improvs from the orchestra, etc.

The Synthetic Theatre (created by Marinetti, Settimelli, Cangiullo, Buzzi, Mario Carli, Folgore, Pratella, Jannelli, Nannetti, Remo Chiti, Mario Dessy, Balla, Volt, Depero, Rognoni, Soggetti, Masnata, Vasari, Alfonso Dolce) has successfully been begun in Italy by the companies Berti, Ninchi, Zoneada, Tumiati, Mateldi, Petrolini, Luciano Molinari; in Paris and Geneva by the avant-guard Society "Art et liberté"; in Prague by the Czechoslovakian company of the Svandovo Theatre.

Our Theatre of Surprise has been represented and begun by the De Angelis Futurist Company before audiences in Naples, Palermo, Rome, Florence, Genoa, Turin, Milan. According to the review of a none too favorable paper, "Il Giorno," the presentations were "frighteningly happy." In Rome, The passéist were extraordinarily insolent and they were beaten up by Marinetti, Cangiullo and the Fornari brothers. The kick in the posterior brain, which the painter Toto Fornari implanted upon a passéist who had climbed on stage to resume his vegetative argument, is legendary. With that surprising kick, Fornari shoved the passéist in a box seat.

The Theatre of Surprise exhibited, in Naples, the paintings of Pasqualino Cangiullo; in Rome, those of Toto Fornari presented by the painter, Balla; in Florence the paintings of Marasco; in Milan those of Bernini.

The Theatre of Surprise begun the "discussions" between pianos, between piano and viola created by the futurist musicians Aldo Mantia, Mario Bartoccini, Vittorio Mortari and Franco Baldi.

THEATRICAL SURPRISES

The Exact Hour — by Cangiullo

Two gentlemen walking meet a third gentleman.

Third (to one of the two): Excuse me, can you tell me the time?
One of the two: I'm sorry, but I'm fast.
Third (to the other one): Can you tell it to me?
The other: Sorry, but I'm slow.
The two of them to the third: Well. . . and you?
The third: I'm neither fast nor slow.
The two: How come?
Third: Because I don't even have it!

(Curtain)

This skit was acted out in the home of Comm. Florio in Palermo. The actor who played the part of the Third gentleman had his wife present in the room at the time along with several friends. These, after the line (I don't even have it!) all spontaneously filed before the wife of the actor to offer her their profound condolences while the wife screamed . . . . wife surprise.

Advise of the draft — by Cangiullo

The wedding crowd (shouting towards the wings): Horray for the wedding couple! Hooraaay!
A professor (entering on the scene): Post-war times and they get married!
A friend of the groom: Not only that, but the groom was discharged for military ineptitude even after the third review of the case.
Professor: Make room there! (exits)
The crowd: Hooray for the married couple!
(Dark on stage)
Head comic, wearing tails: Ladies and gentlemen... what's taking place at this moment... well, think about it...

(stage lights on, it's dawn)

Groom (in suspenders, disheveled, very upset, bumps into his friend)
Friend (alarmed): What's the matter? Where are you going at 5 in the morning? Is there something wrong with your wife?
Groom: Wrong with her? I wish there was! I want a separation!
Friend: How? Already? You've only been united a few hours!
Groom: Time enough to realize that a man like me, declared inept a good three times in his life, cannot be compatible with a woman like her, who in her lifetime has probably many a time been declared extremely skillful. Come on, come with me to the courthouse. (They exit)
Head comic in tails: Ladies and gentlemen, the comedy is finished, as Leoncavallo would say. But if you applaud and call for the actors, we will bring out even the Bride, who, after all, is the real protagonist of this fine little piece.

(down curtain)

Audience: Bring on the bride! Bring on the bride!

(up curtain and the comic repeats his words)

down curtain

Audience: Bring on the bride! Bring on the bride! (Up curtain, and this time the head comic, with a violent effort, drags the bride on stage. She appears finally in a provoking silk nightgown, extremely shy, with her head buried in her folded arms and with two monstrous oranges tied on her belly).

Curtain

The owner of the theatre and the impresario thought that the actress-bride really didn't want to come out before the audience, and they dispatched a legation to the directors of the futurist company demanding that she appear at stage front.

The Public Gardens — by Marinetti & Cangiullo

At the left of the spectator:
A pair of intertwined lovers, sitting on a bench kissing

At the right of the spectators:
A large painting of the Surprise Alphabet, representing 3 wet-nurses by the large letter *B;* each of these suckling a baby in the form of *S.*

— a stereotype queer prances around in feminine movements —

Stage front:
6 passengers in a car (5 men and 1 woman) are seated in the form of a 4, without support of any kind, simulating the bouncing and swaying of a fast moving car, one of the group playing the part of the driver who also imitates all the typical noises of a moving car.

(Curtain)

When this skit was presented in Lucca, as soon as the curtain fell a spectator proceeded to walk on his hands up and down the staircase of the gallery.

In Torino, a spectator masqueraded as Cavour, harrangued the audience by having a debate with another spectator dressed as Mazzini.

Musical "toilette" — Marinetti & Calderone

An upright black piano with a pair of elegant gold lady's shoes inserted on its pedals. The piano's maid dusts the keyboard, abstractly playing the keys with the duster. At the same time, a second maid is busily brushing the "teeth" of the piano with a toothbrush while a hotel flunky dressed in red livery rubs the gold shoes on the piano with a wool cloth.

Curtain

This staged surprise provoked another surprise from the audience. A gentleman, turning to Marinetti, who was seated in a box watching the presentation, shouted: "You people aren't crazy, but you'll drive the rest of us crazy!" At the same instant, from the ballustrade of the balcony, another individual began to whistle violently and then, suddenly, to applaud. The first gentleman then retorted: "There is your first case of insanity" and ran out absolutely terrorized.

Declamation of warlike lyric with tango — by Marinetti

The poet Marinetti recites his Battle in the Fog, excerpt from his novel "L'Alcova d'acciaio" (The Steel Alcove), accompanied by appropriate sounds of bombardments. Two elegant dancers, a man and a woman (he in tails and she in a low cut, rose dress) dance a very languid tango around the orator.

A penetration of the spiritual state of the fighters; mixture of bellicose fury and voluptuousness nostalgia. This declamation, impenetrated with the tango, was also performed as a duet by Marinetti and the Futurist poet Guglielmo Jannelli.

This futurist creation had everywhere—even on the most tumultuous evenings—the prodigious effect of astounding the audience with pathetic admiration, who, after having listened attentively, burst into a roaring ovation.

THEATRICAL SYNTHESES

They are Coming (They Come) — a drama of objects by Marinetti

An elegant room. Night. Large, lighted chandelier. French door, open (in the back, on the left) unto a garden. On the left, along the wall but away from it, a large rectangular table with tablecloth. Along the right wall (where there is a door) a very large, high armchair with 8 chairs, 4 on each side of the armchair.

A Majordomo enters from the door on the left, followed by two servants in tails.

Majordomo: They come. Prepare the room. (exits)

The servants hurriedly arrange the chairs in a semicircle around the armchair, which is not moved and neither is the table. When they finish they gather at the french windows to look, turning their backs to the audience. A long pause. The majordomo reenters, panting.

Majordomo: New orders. They are extremely tired... Bring many pillows, stools... (exits)

The servants go out by the door on the right and soon return loaded with pillows and stools. They take the armchair and place it in the middle of the room. The chairs they arrange in front of the armchair, with their backs to it, 4 on each side. On each chair as well as on the armchair they put pillows and in front of all the chairs and armchair a stool.

The servants again go to the french windows to look out. Long pause.

The majordomo (enters again from the garden, breathless): Another order. They are hungry. Set the table! (exits)

The servants place the table in the middle of the room and arrange the chairs around it, the armchair at the head. Then quickly, coming and going, they set the table. At one place they put a vase of flowers; at another a lot of bread; at another, 8 bottles of wine. At the rest of the places just the silverware. One of the chairs is leaned against the table in the way that one does in a restaurant to signal that the place is reserved. When they are finished, the servants again go to the door to look out. Another long waiting period.

Majordomo (running in): Briccatirakamekame! (gibberish) (exits)

Immediately the servants return the set table to its original place. Then they place the armchair in front of the french windows at an angle, then place the 8 chairs behind it in a straight row but diagonally across the stage. They turn off the chandelier. The room is lit only by the pallor of moonlight which enters from the french windows. A hidden spotlight projects on the floor the shadows of the chairs and the armchair. Conspicuous shadows which (by slowly moving the light) visibly lengthen towards the direction of the door. The servants, huddled in a corner, await trembling, with obvious fear for the chairs to exit from the room.

Curtain

In "They Come," Marinetti wanted to create a drama of objects. All sensitive and imaginative people have surely observed at times the awesome impressions which furniture in general, and chairs and armchairs in particular, suggest in a room void of human presence.

The 8 chairs and the armchair, in the various positions in which they are put during the skit, acquire, little by little, a fantastic life force. At the end, the spectator, with the help of the lengthening shadows which move towards the door, is bound to feel that the chairs are virtually alive and they will move out by themselves.

Simultaneity – a compenetration by Marinetti

A room. The wall on the right is completely taken by bookshelves. A little to the left, a large table. On the left wall, some modest furniture of the kind owned by an unimportant middle class family, and a door. On the back wall, a window which shows that it is snowing outside and another door that opens onto a stairway.

Around the table, under a shaded light which gives out a greenish light, a middle class family is seated. The mothe sews. The father reads a newspaper. The 16 year old son is doing homework as is the 10 year old son. The daughter, 15, sews.

In front of the bookshelves there is a rich and luminous dressing table, with mirror, candelabras, full of bottles and other toilette articles belonging to a very elegant lady. A very bright electric light floods the dressing table where a very beautiful, young coquette, blond and luxuriously robed is seated. She has just finished fixing her hair and is now busy with the finishing touches to the rest of her (face, hands, arms, etc.). She is helped by an attentive and irreproachable maid.

The family does not see this scene.

Mother (to father): You want to look at the bills?

Father: I'll do it later (resumes reading the paper)

Silence. The family continues with its various occupations. The coquette also continues with her make-up unseen by the family. The maid, as if hearing the doorbell, goes to the door on the back wall, opens it, and lets in a delivery boy who goes over to the coquette and delivers a bouquet of flowers and a note. The coquette smells the flowers, puts them on the table and reads the note. The boy exits.

The 16 year old (interrupting his studies and looking out the window): It is still snowing... How quiet it is!

The father: This house is really too isolated. Next year we'll move...

(The coquette's maid goes again to the door and lets in a young milliner who goes toward the coquette and shows her a beautiful hat. She tries it on, looks at herself in the mirror, doesn't like it and puts it aside. Then she gives the milliner a tip and dismisses her.

Suddenly the mother looks for something on the table and stands up and leaves the room by the door on the left, as if to go get something she needs.

The father gets up and goes toward the window and looks outside. Little by little the three children fall asleep at the table. The coquette leaves her dressing table and slowly, cautiously nears the table, takes the bills, the homework, the sewing and throws everything under the table carelessly.)

Coquette: Sleep!
(Then slowly returns to the dressing table and continues to do her nails)

Curtain

In "Simultaneity" Marinetti has staged the simultaneous compenetration of the life of a middle class family and that of a coquette. The coquette, who is not a symbol but a synthesis of luxurious sensations, or disorder, adventure and squandering, exists in the beings of all the persons gathered around the table, either in the form of distress, desire or regret.

The Contract: by Marinetti

Bedroom. Semidark. A white bed can be perceived upon which Mr. Paolo Dami is in agony.

Friend (entering says to the maid): Paola is dying... There is no hope?

Maid: A glimmer of hope. The bullet passed through the lung.

Friend: But tell me... Did he do it because of her?

Maid: Oh, no. Mr. Paolo killed himself for the apartment. I'll explain the enigma to you. Recently he had asked the landlord to open a window that would give him a view of the street. For the great parade, you know... That idiot refused. Three days ago, Mr. Paolo found out that the landlord was discussing the rental of the apartment with a new client. The idea of losing this apartment crazed him with pain and he shot himself!

Paolo Dami (hallucinating): Fire! Fire! The apartment is burning! Call the fire department (calms down).

(Enter doctor and a blond woman, very elegant, dressed in black who goes to the bedside facing the spectators.)
Friend (to doctor): Is there nothing that can be done?

Doctor (gravely): Nothing! You see... the case is very serious... When a gentleman enters an apartment, the case is serious but there is always the hope of getting well... But when an apartment enters the gentleman, the case is really desperate!

(At this moment, the lady goes to the other side of the bed, turning her back to the audience. On her back there is a sign that reads: FOR RENT).

Curtain

APPENDIX C

Tactilism — by Filippo Tommaso Marinetti

Read at the l'Oeuvre, Theatre (Paris), World Exposition of Modern Art (Geneva), and published in the "Comedia" in January, 1921.

Futurism, founded by us in Milan in 1909, gave to the world a hatred for the museum, of the academies and for sentimentalism; it also gave action to art, a defense to youth against all senilisms, the glorification of the original, illogical and insane genius, the artistic sensibility of mechanization, of velocity, of the Variety Theatre and of the simultaneous penetrabilities of modern life, the liberation of words, plastic dynamism, a harmony of noises, the synthetic theatre. Today, Futurism doubles its creative efforts.

Last summer, in Antignano, there, where Amerigo Vespucci Way, the discoverer of America, winds along the sea, I invented Tactilism. On the top of the factories filled with workers, the red flags were waving (my note: communist flags).

I was nude in the silken water which was lacerated by rocks, like frothy scissors, knives, razors, among the mattresses of seaweed impregnated with iodine. I was nude in the sea of flexible steel which had a verile and fecund breath. I was drinking from the cup of the sea which was full of genius unto its edge. The sun with its long, torrid flames vulcanized my body.

A rustic girl, who smelled of salt and warm stone, smiled as she looked at my first tactile board:

"You're amusing yourself by making little boats!"

I answered:

"Yes, I am constructing a craft which will carry the human spirit to unknown neighborhoods."

Here were my reflections as I swam:

The majority of rustic and base men came out of the great war with the sole preoccupation of gaining for themselves the best material comfort possible.

A minority, composed of artists and thinkers, sensitive and refined, manifests, on the other hand, symptoms of a profound and mysterious malady which is probably a result of the great tragic exertion which the war imposed on humanity.

The symptoms of this malady are listlessness, a neurasthenia which is much too feminine, a hopeless pessimism, a febrile indecision of lost instincts and an absolute lack of will.

The rustic and base majority of men throws itself tumultuously into the revolutionary conquest of the communist paradise, and gives a final blow to the problem of happiness in their conviction that it can be resolved by satisfying all the material needs and appetites.

The intellectual minority ironically deprecates this anxious effort, and no longer enjoying the ancient benefits of religion, art and love, which used to constitute its privileges and refuges, views life as a cruel process which it can no longer enjoy, and it abandons itself

89

to unusual pessimism, sexual perversions (or inversions) and to the artificial paradise of cocaine, opium, etc.

The majority and the minority denounce progress, civilization, the mechanical forces of velocity and of the hygienic comforts, in short, Futurism, as being responsible for their past, present and future misfortunes.

Almost all of them proposed a return to the primitive life, contemplative, leisurely, solitary, far from the dreaded cities.

We Futurists, who boldly confront the spasmodic postwar drama, favor all revolutionary attempts by the majority. But to that minority of artists and thinkers we shout in loud voice:

"Life always has meaning! Those artificial paradises with which you try to assassinate it are useless. Stop dreaming of an absurd return to the primitive life. Beware of condemning the superior forces of Society and the wonders of velocity. Concern yourselves, rather, with curing the post-war ills by giving nourishment to humanity in the form of new joys. Rather than destroying human agglomerations, there is a need to perfect them. Intensify the communications and fusions among human beings. Destroy the distances and barriers that separate them in love and friendship. Give full play and total beauty to these two essential manifestations of life: Love and Friendship."

In my careful and antitraditional observations of all the erotic and sentimental phenomenons which unite the two sexes, and of the equally complex phenomenons of friendship, I have learned that human beings speak to each other with the mouth and eyes, but they don't attain a true sincerity due to the insensitivity of the skin, which is even now a mediocre conductor of thought.

While the eyes and the voices communicate their essences, the touch of two individuals communicate almost nothing of their (clash, shock, impact, collision, tiff. The word *urti* pg. 2 par 6, can mean all of these, so take your pick), intrigues or irritations.

Because of this, the necessity of transforming the handshake, the kiss and the coupling into a continuous transmission of thoughts.

I began by subjecting my sense of touch to an intensive treatment, localizing the confused phenomenons of the will and thought upon various points of my body, particularly on the palms of my hands. This training is slow but easy and all healthy bodies can give, through this training, surprising and precise results.

On the other hand, sensibilities which are unhealthy, which derive their excitabilities and their apparent perfection from the bodily weakness itself, will attain the great tactile virtue less easily, without continuity and certainty.

I have created a primary scale to educate the sense of touch, which is at the same time a scale of tactile values for Tactilism, or the Art of the Touch.

Primary scale, plain with 4 different touch categories:

First category: certain, abstract, cold touch
                   sand paper
                   foil (metallic paper, foil paper)

Second category: touch without warmth, persuasive, reasonable or logical
                              smooth silk
                              silk crepe

Third category: exciting, tepid, nostalgic
                              velvet
                              Pyrrenese wool
                              wool
                              silk-wool crepe

Fourth category: almost irritating, warm, volitive
                              grainy silk
                              braided silk
                              spongy material (i.e., cloth)

Secondary scale, of volumes (mass, bulk):

Fifth category: soft, warm, human
                              suede
                              horse hair or dog hair
                              human hair (head and body)
                              Maribu

Sixth category: warm, sensual, affectionate, witty – this has 2 divisions
                              rough iron   "peluche" (material of fake fur)
                              soft brush   fuzz of the meat or peach
                              sponge   bird down
                              iron brush

Through this distinction of tactile values, I have created:

1. Simple tactile tables – which I will present to the public at our conferences on the Art
   of Touch. I have arranged in knowledgeable harmonious or antithetical combinations
   the various tactile values previously catalogued.

2. Abstract or suggestive tactile tables (Journeys of the hands):

   The tactile table has an arrangement of tactile values which permit the hands to wander
   over them following colored tracks thus realizing an unfolding or suggestive sensations
   whose rhythm at times languid, cadenced or tumultuous is regulated by precise instruc-
   tions.

      One of these abstract tactile tables created by me and called "Sudan-Paris" contain in
   the "Sudan" part certain tactile values which are rough, greasy, rough, pungent, searing
   (spongy material, sponge, sand paper, wool, brush, iron brush); in the part called "Sea"
   there are tactile values which are slippery, metallic, cool (silver foil); in the "Paris" part,
   tactile values which are soft, extremely delicate, fondling, warm and cold at once (silk,
   velvet, feathers, down puffs).

3. Tactile tables for the different sexes:

In these tactile tables, the arrangement of the tactile values allows the hands of a man and those of a woman, in tune with each other, to follow and evaluate together their tactile journey.

These tactile tables are extremely varied, and the pleasure they give is enriched by the unexpected, in the emulation of two rival sensibilities which will exert themselves in their efforts to feel better and to explain better their concurrent sensations.

These tactile tables are destined to substitute the stupefying game of chess.

4. Tactile pillows.

5. Tactile couches.

6. Tactile beds.

7. Tactile clothing.

8. Tactile rooms.

In the tactile rooms the floors and walls will be huge tactile tables. Tactile values of mirrors, flowing waters, stones, metals, brushes, very low voltage electric wires, marble, velvets, carpeting which will give pleasurable sensations to barefoot dancers.

We will have theatres predisposed to Tactilism. The seated spectators will place their hands on running tactile tapes which produce tactile sensations of various rhythms. These tapes can also be mounted on small reels, accompanied by music and lights.

9. Tactile tables for improvisations "freewords":
The tactilist will audibly express the tactile sensations received by the journey of his hands. His improvisation will be "freeword," (that is, free from prosody or syntax) essential and synthetic improvisation, and as unlike human as possible...

The tactilist may be blindfolded but it would be preferable to envelop him in the lights of a projector. The novices will be blindfolded who have not as yet trained their tactile sensitivity.

For the accomplished tactilists, the full lights of a projector are preferable, since darkness has the drawback of concentrating the sensibility into an excessive abstract.

Education for the Sense of Touch:

1. The hands must be gloved for many days during which time the brain will instill in the hands a desire for the different tactile sensations.

2. Swim underwater, in the sea, in an effort to tactily distinguish the currents and different temperatures.

3. Enumerate and identify every night, in total darkness, all the objects in the bedroom. My first tactile experiments were in fact made by means of this exercise in a dark trench in Gorizia in 1917.

I have never pretended to have invented tactile sensitivity, which has already manifested itself in ingenious forms in the *Jongleuse* and in the *Hors-nature* of Rachilde. Other artists and writers have had the presentiment of tactilism. There has existed, moreover, for a long time an art of the plastic touch. My good friend Boccioni, futuristic painter and sculptor, felt tactically while creating in 1911 his plastic piece Fusion of a Head and of a Window using contrasting materials in both tactile value and weight: iron, porcelain and woman's hair.

The Tactilism created by me is an art distinctly different from the plastic arts. It has nothing to do with or gain from painting or sculpture and everything to lose by them.

In the tactile tables one must avoid, as much as possible, a variety of colors, for they lend themselves to plastic impressions. Painters and sculptors tend to naturally subordinate tactile values to visual values therefore they will find it difficult to create significant tactile tables. Tactilism it seems to me is reserved particularly for young poets, pianists, typists and to all those with refined and potent erotic temperaments.

Tactilism, nevertheless, must avoid collaboration not only with the plastic arts but also morbose erotomania. It must aim towards tactile harmony and indirectly collaborate to perfect spiritual communication between human beings through the epidermis. The distinction of the five senses is arbitrary and someday surely numerous other senses will be uncovered and catalogued. Tactilism will favor this discovery.

APPENDIX D

FUTURIST MANIFESTO

Filippo Tommaso Marinetti and Bruno Corra (1923-1924)

Against dead theatre
Against the analytical novel (or Romance)
Against musical *negrism* (Death)

Our smiling summer unfortunately signaled a return to the past which manifested itself with tedious presentations of dead outdoor theatre.

With the exception of a few masterpieces such as Romagnoli's *Oedipus Rex* we condemn this literary necrophilia in the rejuvenating period of Imperial Italy projected by the Duce (Mussolini).

Enough of ancient ruins, shouts of Agamemnon, lamentations of Egisto, cries of Clitemnestra, misfortunes of the Atridi, speeches of the Seven Against Thebes administered to a public yawning in a swamp of boredom.

Mildew, yawns, stretching of arms and no one understands why the personages on stage are so despairing.

Anxious dialogues of the spectators: "Who is that one over there?" "What is that one doing?" "What's happened to that old bearded one?"

Our archeological theatrical people avail themselves of an expression of the Duce which they have interpreted to suit themselves "Theatre of the Masses" "To go towards the people":

1. For some time the Duce clarified everything by declaring the need to construct theatres capable of holding comfortably thousands of people, a cash intake based on prices which would be no hardship even for the most humble social classes.

2. On the other hand, nothing is further from the masses of spectators than the presentations of this dead theatre which presupposes a scholarly knowledge in the small business man, the worker and the peasant.

3. Our archeological theatrical people and those who talk about reinstating a state of health to the theatre by taking it outdoors fall into that old illusion of resolving existing difficulties by returning to the "ancient," forgetting that today's presentations (or shows) leave the public dissatisfied because they are not modern enough and therefore boringly static in theatres without a revolving stage.

4. We deny that the ancient ampitheatre can host a modern theatrical work or inspire an author to an original drama unless there is the stimulating possibility of writing for a theatre which is accurately constructed to be electro-mechanic. We might add that however inadequate modern theatres may be, they are not as inadequate as centuries old ruins.

5. The presentations of the dead theatre—a combination of cultural exhibitionism and an aristocratic snobbism which is out of phase with a simple, rapid, plebeian and great fascist Italy—are unrealistic and detrimental to the public and the authors and especially to the actors who, in specializing in the vocal bombardments of the Greco-Romans become trombones, losing concentration, relaxation and incisiveness.

6. Producers who think to uncover, amidst the rustic and barbaric jumble of primitive personages who walk about amidst wailing choruses and bat-like drapery nailed to the walls, material suited to their ambitions, rather than looking for it in a perfect theatre of our perfect urbanization, are way off base.

7. The influence of the movie maker on the theatre is providential in that it keeps it from indulgence and from receding, but forces it towards progress since every day the public renews its sensibility in the movie houses.

8. A separation must be made between the terms which have been equivocally united: "classical performance" and "outdoor theatre," since the latter, if equipped with a perfected stage set among plants and flowers becomes one of our ideals of summertime pleasures, totally modern.

In conclusion, the production of a dead theatre shows signs of foreign influences and its style, imprinted with an asexual aestheticism, is of a foreign brand derived from the illustrious and extremely boring (bothersome can also be used) Max Reinhardt.

We transfigurators and creators of new realities, friends of the tacit (implicit) synthesis, condemn analytical novels which ignore the indispensible originality of conception, the indispensible inventiveness of characterization and the indispensible choice of suggestive words and gestures by pedantically anatomizing any life of any idiot in an ambient rendered ordinary (nondescript) by the lack of selective genius.

In order to sell their books to readers who, in recompense for the money spent on it want as large and long a book as possible, novelists adopt the cold, gray cloud cover (i.e., meaning style) descendant from the North (i.e., Germany) which favors the dramatization of remorse and gossip worthy of a street beggar while they (novelists) suffocate our lively conciseness and dynamic Italian narrative art form under an endless, stupefying psychology.

These imitators and exaggerators of the "interior monologue" and "asides" of old comedies, with their long Freudian regurgitations of banalities—may they be relegated to the Pharmacologea as sleeping pills guaranteed to work, prescribed with caution.

As to the living Italian musicians and those living creators of our comedy—we are equally battling in the funeral humor, also derived from the North, and the funeral asthma of what might be called musical negrism obstinately dreary, interrupted by songs and dances with the rhythmic movement of a piston, from which we have hoped for 25 years, and hope no more, to see the flower of originality bud.

Instead, monotony weighs heavy in concert halls, balls and dinner dances where everyone contemplates suicide when the conductor, thinking that he is renewed by the lack of his conductors rod, abandons himself to spastic gestures to put in motion the false cheerfulness of the musicians.

Enough, enough, enough.

Rather let's cheer the "tarantella" (Italian folkdance and music) with its virile musical instruments from the Bay of Naples.

Let's hear it for the "tofa," a large shell which makes a tragicomic sound in mockery of mythology, sirens and tritons.

Let's hear it for the "caccavella," a clay bowl covered with a skin with a stick inserted in it which, when rubbed with a wet hand, makes a humorous noise to mock the moonlight.

Let's hear it for the "scetavaisse," an arc of wood covered with pieces of sheet metal, genial instrument of parody of the virtuoso and of the conservatories.

Let's hear it for the "Triccabballacche," a sheet of wood whose strings are made of very fine strips of wood which end in little square hammer heads. It is played like cymbals.

All of these played with spontaneous joy, in scorn of the morbid musical negrism and the depressing, plaintive tangos.

NOTES

SECTION I

1. Robert W. Flint, *Marinetti: Selected Writings* (New York: Farrar, Straus and Giroux, 1972), pp. 9-10.

2. Ibid., p. 11.

3. Ibid., p. 12.

4. Whore house.

5. Risorgimenti—reawakening—a term used to describe Italy's artistic regeneration in the second half of the nineteenth century.

6. Salvatore Saladino, *Italy from Unification to 1919* (New York: Thomas Y. Crowell Co., 1970), pp. 104-121.

7. Filippo Tommaso Marinetti, *Teatro F.T. Marinetti,* ed. Giovanni Calendoli (Rome: Vito Bianco Editore, 1960), III, pp. 17-20.

8. Filippo Tommaso Marinetti, "Foundation Manifesto," *Le Figaro* (Feb. 20, 1909), p. 1.

9. City life.

10. James Joll, *Intellectual in Politics* (London: Weidenfeld and Nicolson, 1960), pp. 135-136.

11. Jane Raye, *Futurism* (New York: E.P. Dutton, 1972), p. 11.

12. Passèism is the term used by the Futurists for all attitudes, philosophies, art and politics which were not Futurist.

13. Giovanni Papini, *L'Esperienza Futurista* (Firenze: Vallecchi, 1919), pp. 56-58.

14. William Askew, *Europe and Italy's Acquisition of Libya, 1911-1912* (Durham: Univ. Press, 1942), pp. 66-81.

15. Filippo Marinetti, "Address to the Tripolitans," *Selected Writings,* trans. R. W. Flint (New York: Farrar, Straus and Giroux, 1972), pp. 83-84.

16. A. Rossi, *The Rise of Italian Fascism* (Oxford: Clarendon Press, 1938), pp. 79-126.

17. Oberdau—a young radical who tried to assassinate the Austrian Emperor.

18. Joll, *Intellectual Life in Politics,* p. 38.

19. Marinetti, "Banish the Moonlight," *Selected Writings,* trans. R.W. Flint (New York: Farrar, Straus and Giroux, 1972), pp. 109-110.

20. Giovanni Papini, *L'Esperienza Futurista* (Firenze: Vallecchi, 1919), p. 3.

21. Marinetti, "War The World's Only Hygiene," *Selected Writings,* trans. R.W. Flint (New York: Farrar, Straus and Giroux, 1972), pp. 270-271.

22. Marinetti, "War The World's Only Hygiene," *Selected Writings,* trans. R.W. Flint (New York: Farrar, Straus and Giroux, 1972), p. 272.

23. Benedetto Croce, *Estetica Come Scienza dell'espressione e Linguistica Generale* (Firenze: Vallecchi, 1924), p. 5.

SECTION II

1. There are numerous translations of this manifesto. Selection of this translation by Robert Brain was for its clarity and coherence.

2. Umberto Boccioni, Carlo Carrà, Luigi Russolo, Giocomo Balla, Gino Severini, "Manifesto of the Futurist Painters," trans. Robert Brain, *The Documents of 20th Century Art: Futurist Manifestos* (New York: Viking Press, 1973), pp. 24-27.

3. Carlo Carrà, Umberto Boccioni, Luigi Russolo, Giacomo Balla, Gino Severini, "Exhibitors to the Public," *Exhibition of Works of the Italian Futurist Painters* (London: Sackville Gallery, 1912), pp. 2-15.

4. Giacomo Balla, "The Late Balla–Futurist Balla," trans. Caroline Tisball, *The Documents of 20th Century Art: Futurist Manifestos* (New York: Viking Press, 1973), p. 206.

5. Carlo Carrà, Umberto Boccioni, Luigi Russolo, Giacomo Balla, Gino Severini, "Exhibitors to the Public," *Exhibition of Works of the Italian Futurist Painters* (London: Sackville Gallery, 1912), pp. 2-15.

6. Umberto Boccioni, "Pittura Scultura Futuriste," *Poesia* (1914), pp. 6-9.

7. Umberto Boccioni, *Opera Completa* (Foligno: Campitelli, 1927), p. 39.

8. Umberto Boccioni, "Pittura Scultura Futuriste," *Poesia* (1914), pp. 6-9.

9. Umberto Boccioni, "Pittura Scultura Futuriste," *Poesia* (1914), pp. 6-9.

10. Umberto Boccioni, Carlo Carrà, Luigi Russolo, Giacomo Balla, Gino Severini, "Manifesto of the Futurist Painters," trans. Robert Brain, *The Documents of 20th Century Art: Futurist Manifestos* (New York: Viking Press, 1973), pp. 24-27.

11. Umberto Boccioni, Carlo Carrà, Luigi Russolo, Giacomo Balla, Gino Severini, "Exhibitors to the Public," *Exhibition of Works of the Italian Futurist Painters* (London: Sackville Gallery, 1912), p. 7.

12. Umberto Boccioni, Carlo Carrà, Luigi Russolo, Giacomo Balla, Gino Severini, "Manifesto of the Futurist Painters," trans. Robert Brain, *The Documents of 20th Century Art: Futurist Manifestos* (New York: Viking Press, 1973), pp. 24-27.

13. Ardengo Soffici, "Cubismo e Futurismo," *La Voce* (March 23, 1914), pp. 12-15.

14. Umberto Boccioni, "Pittura Scultura Futuriste," *Poesia* (1914), pp. 6-9.

15. Carlo Carrà, "Pittura Metafiscca," *Poesia* (1913), p. 5.

16. Umberto Boccioni, Carlo Carrà, Luigi Russolo, Giocomo Balla, Gino Severini, "Manifesto of the Futurist Painters," trans. Robert Brain, *The Documents of 20th Century Art: Futurist Manifestos* (New York: Viking Press, 1973), pp. 24-27.

17. Ardengo Soffici, "Cubismo e Futurismo," *La Voce* (March 23, 1914), pp. 12-15.

18. Umberto Boccioni, "Pittura Scultura Futiste," *Poesia,* (1914), pp. 6-9.

19. Carlo Carrà, "Pittura Metafiscca," *Poesia* (1913), p. 7.

20. After first savagely attacking the show, Apollinaire relented and published a column of partial appreciation with reservations. Probably Marinetti was able to intervene on behalf of the painters as he and Apollinaire were old friends.

21. Carlo Carrà, "Futurist Painting: Technical Manifesto," *Exhibition of Works of the Italian Futurist Painters* (London: Sackville Gallery, 1912), pp. 6-12.

22. Filippo Marinetti, "The Pleasure of Being Booed," *War the World's Only Hygiene,* trans. R.W. Flint (New York: Straus, Giroux, and Farnac, 1972), pp. 219-224.

SECTION III

1. John Gassner, *Theatre in our Times* (New York: Crown Publishers, 1954), p. 7.

2. Mordecai Gorelik, *New Theatres for Old* (New York: E.P. Dutton Co., 1962), pp. 256-257.

3. No adequate material has yet been made available on the extent to which the Fascists manipulated the Futurists.

4. A 'serate,' loosely translated, meant an evening of readings, declamations, riots, music and whatever else could be brought into the scenario. A 'serate' was attended by an audience, no matter how small.

5. A passatista was an old fashioned, conservative, passé person; it was also anyone who did not agree with the Futurist view.

6. Francesco Cangiullo, "La Battaglia di Firenze," *Sipario* (Dec., 1967), p. 29.

7. The manifestos selected for inclusion in the text demonstrate the development of Futurist theory between 1913 and 1933. Not all have previously been available in English. Moreover, much of the feeling and tone of the movement is best acquired from reading these documents.

8. Filippo Tommaso Marinetti, "Variety Theatre Manifesto," *Lacerba* (October, 1913), pp. 1-7.

9. F.T. Marinetti, "Variety Theatre Manifesto," *Lacerba* (October, 1913), p. 5.

10. F.T. Marinetti, "Foundation Manifesto," *Le Figaro* (February 20, 1909), p. 3.

11. F.T. Marinetti, "Les Mots en Liberté Futuristes," *Poesia* (December, 1919), p. 42.

12. Ardengo Soffici, *Primi Principii di Una Estetica Futurista* (Firenze: Vallecchi, 1920), p. 41.

13. Umberto Boccioni, "Pittura Scultura Futuriste," *Poesia* (January, 1914), p. 211.

14. F.T. Marinetti, "Les Mots en Liberté Futuristes," *Poesia* (December, 1919), p. 42.

15. Evidence suggests that musical indications also served to direct the vocalizing of some plays and poems and to indicate additional instrumental accompaniment.

16. F.T. Marinetti, "Les Mots en Liberté Futuristes," *Poesia* (December, 1919), p. 43.

17. Marinetti refers to the "verbal alchemy" of certain French writers and to Mallarmé's practice of emphasizing certain phrases by setting them in larger type.

18. F.T. Marinetti, "I Poeti Futuristi," *Poesia* (March, 1912), p. 6.

19. Ardengo Soffici, *Primi Principii di una Estetica Futurista* (Firenze: Vallecchi, 1920), p. 87.

20. Craig's magazine, *The Mask,* was published in Florence from 1906-1912. The Futurists had read his articles.

21. F.T. Marinetti, *Drama Senza Titolo* (Firenze: Vallecchi, 1915), pp. 6-7.

22. Carlo Carrà, "The Futurist Soirées," *Art and the Stage in the Twentieth Century,* ed. Henning Rischbieter (Greenwich: New York Graphic Soc., Ltd., 1968), p. 74.

23. F.T. Marinetti, "The Variety Theatre Manifesto," *Lacerba* (October, 1913), p. 6.

24. Benedetto Croce was an Italian philosopher of international repute.

25. Michael Kirby, *Futurist Performance* (New York: E.P. Dutton, 1971), p. 28.

26. Maria Drudi Gambillo and Teresa Fiori (eds.) *Archivi del Futurismo,* 2 vols. (Rome: DeLuca Editore, 1958), p. 38.

27. Maria Drudi Gambillo and Teresa Fiori (eds.) *Archivi del Futurismo,* 2 vols. (Rome: DeLuca Editore, 1958), p. 39.

28. F.T. Marinetti, "Futurism and the Theatre," *The Mask* (January, 1914), pp. 188-193.

29. For a full discussion of Futurist music and 'bruitisme' (noise music) see Luigi Russolo, *The Art of Noise.*

30. F.T. Marinetti, Emilio Settimelli, Bruno Corra, "The Futurist Synthetic Theatre" (Milano: Instituto Editoriale, January, 1915).

31. F.T. Marinetti, Emilio Settimelli, Bruno Corra, "The Futurist Synthetic Theatre" (Milano: Instituto Editoriale, January, 1915), p. 7.

32. F.T. Marinetti, Emilio Settimelli, Bruno Corra, "The Futurist Synthetic Theatre" (Milano: Instituto Editoriale, January, 1915), p. 2.

33. Angelo Rognoni, *Education,* translated by Victoria Nes Kirby, from *Futurist Performance* by Michael Kirby (New York: Dutton Co., 1971), p. 301.

34. F.T. Marinetti, Emilio Settimelli, Bruno Corra, "The Futurist Synthetic Theatre" (Milano: Instituto Editoriale, January, 1915), p. 5.

35. These devices were in use as training methods for actors.

36. A standard technique employed by Commedia Dell'Arte and Vaudeville.

37. F.T. Marinetti, Emilio Settimelli, Bruno Corra, "The Futurist Synthetic Theatre" (Milano: Instituto Editoriale, January, 1915), p. 6.

38. This term is fully described in Section II of this study.

39. Enrico Prampolini, "Futurist Scenography," *Der Futurismus* no. 4, (August, 1922), p. 10. This manifesto was written in April 1915.

40. These costumes may not have been built but others which utilized the concepts were constructed.

41. Edited manuscript.

42. Depero refers to kinetic sculpture done in 1915.

43. Michael Kirby, *Futurist Performance* (New York: E.P. Dutton Co., 1971), pp. 83-86.

44. Maxim Gordon, "The Italian Futurists," *Theatre Magazine* (September, 1925), p. 61.

45. Enrico Prampolini, "The Magnetic Theatre and the Futurist Scenic Atmosphere," *The Little Review* (Winter, 1926), pp. 101-108.

46. F.T. Marinetti, *Total Theatre Manifesto,* trans. Paola Martini.

SELECTED
BIBLIOGRAPHY

Books

Apollonio, Umberto. *Pittura Moderna Italiana*. Venezia: Nori Pozza, 1950.

Askew, William. *Europe and Italy's Acquisition of Libya, 1911-1912*. Durham: University Press. 1942.

Azari, Fedèle. "Theatre Aerien Futuriste." *Roma Futurista*, January 18, 1920.

Balla, Guido. *Pittori Italiani dal Futurismo a Oggi*. Firenze: Edizioiu Mediterranee, 1956.

Banham, Roger. "Futurism and Modern Architecture," in *Royal Institute of British Architects Journal*. London, Vol. 64, February, 1957.

Barr, Alfred H. and Soby, Thrall J. *Twentieth Century Italian Art*. New York: Museum of Modern Art, 1949.

Boccioni, Umberto. *Opere Complete a Cura di F.T. Marinetti*. Foligno: Campitelli, 1927.

——— . *Pittura Scultura Futuriste*. Milano: Edizioni Futuriste di "Poesia," 1914.

Bragaglia, Antonio. *La Maschera Mobile*. Foligno: Franco Campitelli, 1926.

Cangiullo, Francesco. *Caffe Concerto*. Milano. Edizioni Futuriste di "Poesia," 1919.

——— . *Le Serate Futuriste*. Naples: 1930. Republished, Milan: Casa Editrice Ceschina, 1961.

Carrieri, R. *Avant-garde Painting and Sculpture in Italy (1890-1955)*. Milano: Instituto Editoriale Dormus, 1955.

Clough, Rosa Trillo. *Futurism: The Story of a Modern Art Movement, a New Appraisal*. New York: The Philosophical Library, 1961.

Croce, Benedetto. *Breviario di Estatica*. Bari: Laterza, 1913.

Durgnat, Raymond. "Futurism and the Movies," *Art and Artists*. February, 1964, pp. 10-15.

Fagiolo dell'Arco, Maruizio. "Balla's Prophecies," *Art International*. Summer, 1968, pp. 63-68.

Falgoi, Enrico. *Il Futurismo—Il Novecentismo*. Torino: I.L.T.E., 1953.

Flint, R.W. *Marinetti, Selected Writings*. New York: Farrar, Straus and Giroux, 1972.

Gambillo, Maria Drudi, and Fiori, Teresa (eds.). *Archivi del Futurismo*. 2 vols. Rome: De Luca Editore, 1958 (Vol. I) and 1962 (Vol. 2).

Gidieon, Seigrid. *Space, Time and Architecture*. Cambridge: Harvard University Press, 1954.

Gordon, Maxim. "The Italian Futurists," *Theatre Magazine*. September, 1925.

Joll, James. *Intellectual in Politics*. London: Weidenfeld and Nicolson, 1960.

Kirby, E.T. *Total Theatre*. New York: E.P. Dutton and Company, Inc., 1969.

Kirby, Michael. *Futurist Performance*. New York, E.P. Dutton Co., 1971.

Marinetti, Filippo Tommaso. "Futurism and the Theatre," *The Mask*. January, 1914.

——— . *Futurism to 1933*. Chicago Tribune, Italian Supplement, 1933.

——— . *Teatro F.T. Marinetti*. ed. Giovanni Calendoli. 3 vols. Rome: Vito Bianco Editore, 1960.

Martin, Marianne W. *Futurist Art and Theory 1909-1915*. Oxford: Clarendon Press, 1968.

Papini, Giovanni. *L'Esperienza Futurista, 1913-1914*. Florence: Vallecchi, 1919. Second Edition 1927.

Prampolini, Enrico. "Il primato Italiano della Scenotechica Futurista," *Mediterraneo Futurista*. Rome, October 1942.

Raye, Jane. *Futurism*. New York: E.P. Dutton, 1972.

Rischbieter, Henning. *Art and The Stage in the Twentieth Century,* ed. H. Rischbieter. Greenwich, Conn: New York Graphic Society, Ltd., 1968.
Rossi, A. *The Rise of Italian Fascism.* Clarendon: Oxford, 1938.
Russolo, Luigi. *L'arte dei Rumovi.* Milano: Edizioni Futuriste di "Poesia," 1916.
_____. "Psofarmoni," *The Little Review.* Winter, 1926, pp. 51-52.
Saladino, Salvatore. *Italy from Unification to 1919.* New York: Thomas Y. Crowell Co., 1970.
Settimelli, Eestague. *Marinetti, L'Uomo e L'Artista.* Milano: Edizioni Futuriste di "Poesia," 1921.
Severini, Giovanni. *Du Cubisme au Classicisme.* Paris Povolozky, 1922.
Soffici, Ardengo. *BIF&Z +18: Simultaneita e Chimismi Lirici.* Firenze: Vallechi, 1919.
_____. *Primi principii di una Estetica Futurista.* Firenze: Vallecchi, 1920.
Taylor, Joshua C. *Futurism.* New York: The Museum of Modern Art, 1961.
Venturi, Leonello. "Introduction to the Exhibition on Prampolini," in *Prampolini,* New York, World House Galleries, 1959.

Periodicals

Cahiers d'Art. Paris: Editions Cahiers d'Arts, 1950.
Lacerba. Florence: Giovanni Papini, 1913-1915.
Il Leonardo. Firenze: Giovanni Papini and Giuseppe Prezzolini, 1903-1907.
Il Regno. Florence: Enrico Corradini, 1903-1906.
La Voce. Firenze: Giuseppe Prezzolini, 1908-1916.

INDEX

Note: those figures in brackets represent the actual text of referenced script or manifesto; page numbers in boldface indicate illustrations.